Tatting Patterns

Lessons & Patterns for Tatting
A Collection of Old Fashioned Fun

TATTING PATTERNS - LESSONS & PATTERNS FOR TATTING WITH INSTRUCTIONS - A COLLECTION OF OLD FASHIONED FUN

First edition. June 5, 2024.

Copyright © 2024 Timeless Digital Publishing.

ISBN: 979-8227209948

Written by Timeless Digital Publishing.

Welcome!

Your search is over for Vintage Tatting Patterns!

This book was created for every person and soul who would love to learn tatting and create things with vintage patterns. These patterns are extremely old and the instructions for some of these patterns may be slightly different than the wording used in today's patterns. All of the directions and instructions have been left as these patterns were originally done – some hundreds of years ago.

Unique and rare, these patterns have been researched and pulled together from numerous books and brought to you here all in one place!

Pour yourself a favorite beverage, sit back, and enjoy!

TATTING INSTRUCTIONS

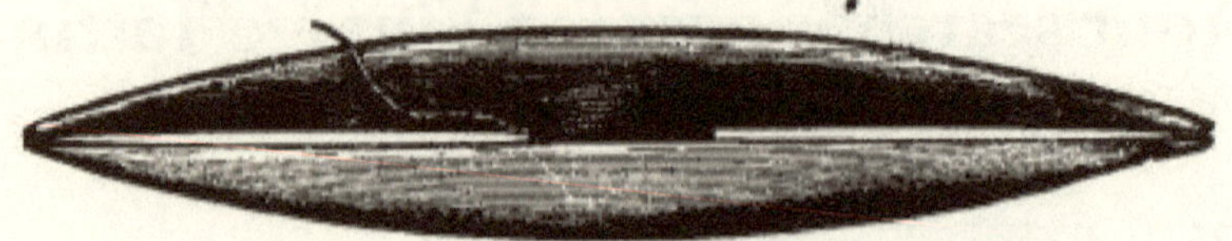

Tatting Shuttle.

The needlework called Tatting in England, *Frivolité* in French, and *Frivolitäten* in German, is a work which seems, from all accounts, to have been in favour several generations ago. Modern ingenuity has discovered some ways of improving on the original plan of tatting, which was, indeed, rather a primitive sort of business as first practised. To Mrs. Mee, one of our most accomplished *artistes* in all matters connected with the work-table, belongs, we believe, the introduction of the plan of working from the reel instead of the shuttle. By this alteration the advantage of the shuttle being constantly kept filled with cotton was gained, and the necessity also obviated for frequently joining the thread; and to Mdlle. Riego, equally distinguished in all details appertaining to the employment of the needle, ladies are indebted for an arrangement by which the same thread used in the making of the pattern is used for fastening the work. The old plan only provided for the working of the different portions which constituted the pattern, and then these portions had to be sewn together with a needle and thread. The ingenious workers on the Continent have also given much attention of late to the art of tatting, and our instructions now printed comprise what we consider the best mode of learning and doing this exceedingly interesting and fashionable work.

Tatting Pin.

Tatting differs entirely from crochet, and is composed of stitches forming *knots*. It is intended as an imitation of point lace, and is especially used for trimming under-linen, on account of its strength.

To make the stitches or knots a small instrument is used, called a *shuttle*. This shuttle consists of two oval pieces, flat on one side and convex on the other, and is made of wood or ivory.

The two oval pieces are joined together by a strong cross-piece. The illustration shows the construction of the shuttle. These shuttles are made in ivory, pearl, tortoiseshell inlaid with pearl, and silver; they are also manufactured in coloured bone, black, red, and white. The best to work with are the pearl for a white shuttle, and the inlaid tortoiseshell for a black shuttle; the prices vary from sixpence to one shilling and two-and-sixpence each. In selecting a shuttle be careful to see that the ends close, as if dropped it soon becomes unthreaded, which is very inconvenient. The cotton intended for the work is wound round this shuttle, and the thickness of the cotton varies according to the style of work. It is better to use the proper tatting cotton, because it is stronger than the ordinary kinds; this is manufactured by Messrs. Walter Evans and Co. for the purpose. Their Boar's Head Cotton is also frequently used, and answers very well.

Shuttles.

These are made in 3 sizes:—Finest, No. 1; No. 2, useful medium size; No. 3, the largest.

The Way to Hold the Hands.

Take the shuttle in the right hand, between the thumb and second finger, and allow the forefinger to remain at liberty, and rest the under part of the shuttle *between* the second and third and *on* the middle finger. Place the thread round the three middle fingers of the left hand, so as to form a loop, keeping the second and third fingers a little apart, and bring the cotton again between the thumb and forefinger, letting the end fall within the palm of the hand, while the end of cotton which holds on to the shuttle passes over the thumb-nail.

To Make a Stitch.

Keep the hands in the position above described; pass the shuttle at the back, through the loop—that is, between the second and third fingers. Take the end of the shuttle which comes out from the loop between the forefinger and thumb of the right hand, and strain the cotton very tightly towards the right. When the cotton is drawn through the loop, this cotton must not be impeded by the fourth finger; it should, on the contrary, slide over it, and be drawn tight. It should divide the loop into two parts. After this withdraw the second left-hand finger, which is *above* the cotton, and pass it again under that cotton, so as to draw up the loop. A *half-stitch* is thus formed, and must be tightened by being drawn closely to the forefinger and thumb of the left hand.

For the remaining half of the stitch keep the hands in the same position, but, instead of letting the cotton fall over the thumb, pass this cotton over the back of the hand; then let the shuttle fall between the second and third fingers of the left hand, in front, and take it out again at the back, strain the cotton very tightly, withdraw the second finger from the loop, letting the cotton which is behind the hand sweep over the fingers. When this is done, guide with the unoccupied fingers of the left hand this second half-stitch up to the other, thus completing *one stitch*.

The Way to Make a Loop in Tatting.

When a certain number of stitches are made, very tightly draw in the loop by straining the cotton until the first stitch touches the last, and thus a loop is formed. During this process the stitches should be held tightly between the forefinger and thumb.

The Way to Make a Purl.

A *purl* is a small loop of cotton often used as an edging in tatting, as, for instance, round the outer edge of the ovals in tatted insertion No. 2. The following is the easiest method of making a purl:—The stitches are not made quite closely together at the place where a purl is to be made; about one-sixth of an inch is left between each. This space is left free until the loop is made by uniting the stitches; then the small piece of cotton in the space bulges out between the stitches, and forms the purl. If several are required a small space is left between every two or three stitches, according to the desired number. Care must be taken in that case that the small pieces of cotton left be all of the same length, so that the purl may be perfectly even. The purl can also be made thus: At the same time with the end of thread take the tatting-pin or a very large darning needle or knitting needle in the left hand, so that the point may come out farther than the row of stitches; if then you wish to make a purl, throw the cotton on the pin before making the stitch; then fasten this stitch, and push it at once close to the preceding; the pin with the cotton should come above the stitches. Do not take out the pin before all the purl and all the stitches are completed and joined together.

Joining the Work.

Place the tatting-pin in the loop that is to be joined, and with the hook draw the thread of the loop—that is, round the hand through it—pass the shuttle through this loop, and draw it up tightly close to the stitches.

A "straight" or double thread is used to join various parts of the work, and forms very beautiful patterns. Without the straight thread we should be unable to imitate point lace patterns, or, indeed, to execute any designs but those composed of circles, ovals, &c. To use this straight thread 2 shuttles are required; they should be of different colours. Sometimes one end of thread is left attached to the reel instead of using the second shuttle. In commencing a loop the straight thread is held between the second and third fingers of the left hand, about 2 or 3 inches from the work; the other shuttle is held as usual in the right hand, and the stitches and purls worked with it upon the foundation of the straight thread of the second shuttle.

First position of the hands (fig. 486).—The construction of the knots or stitches, appears at first sight to present great difficulties but will be easily mastered by attention to the indications here given. One thing, to be constantly borne in mind is, that when the right hand has passed the shuttle through the loop, it must stop with a sudden jerk and hold the thread tightly extended until the left hand has drawn up the knot. After filling the shuttle, take the end of the thread between the thumb and forefinger of the left hand, and the shuttle in the right, pass the thread over the third and fourth fingers of the left hand, bring it back towards the thumb and cross the two threads under the fingers, as indicated in fig. 486. Pass the thread that comes from the shuttle round the little finger of the right hand, and give the shuttle the direction shown in the engraving.

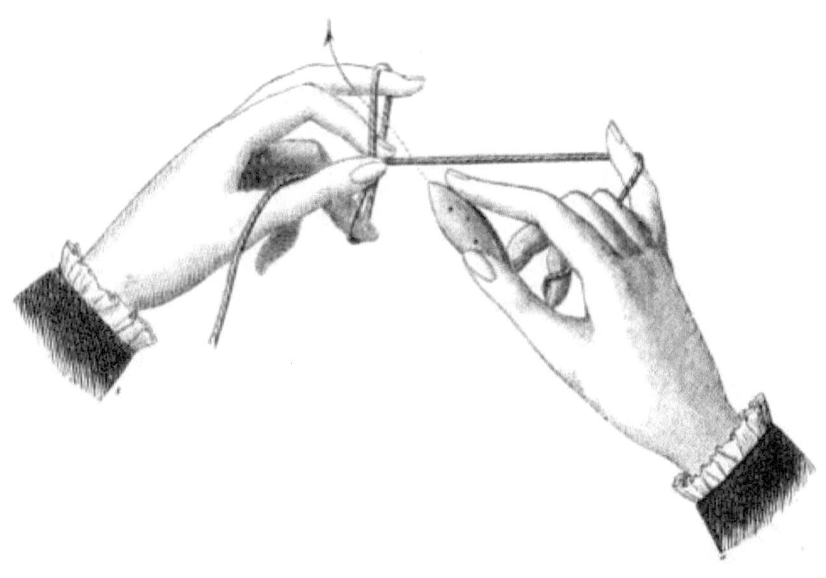

Fig. 486. First position of the hands.

Second and third position of the hands (figs. 487 and 488).—Make the shuttle pass between the first and third fingers, in the direction indicated by the arrow in fig. 487, and bring it out behind the loop.

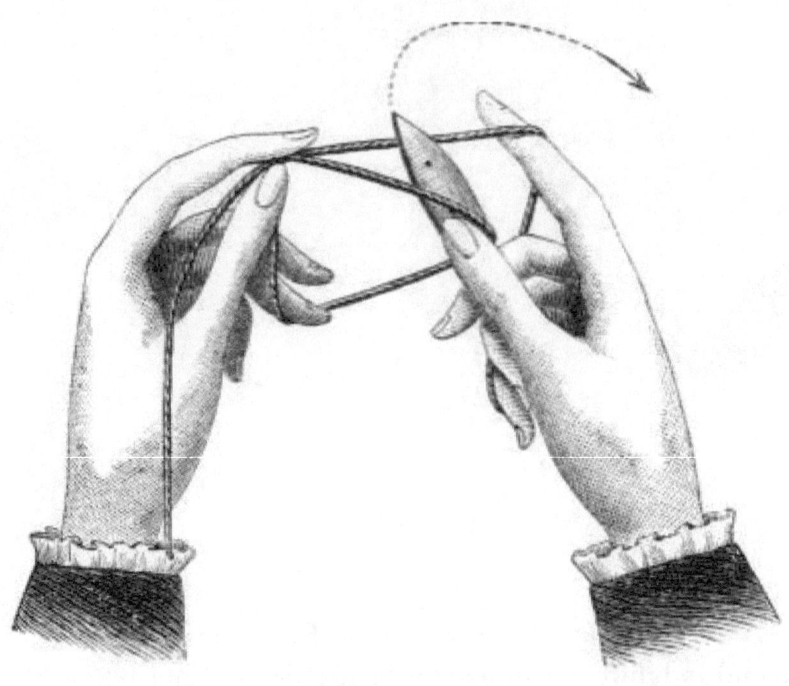

Fig. 487. Second position of the hands.
Here the first difficulties for beginners arise and until they have
sufficiently mastered the movements of both hands not to confuse
them, we advise them to pay careful attention to the following
instructions. As soon as you have put the shuttle through the loop,
place the right hand on the table with the thread tightly extended,
leaving the left hand perfectly passive.

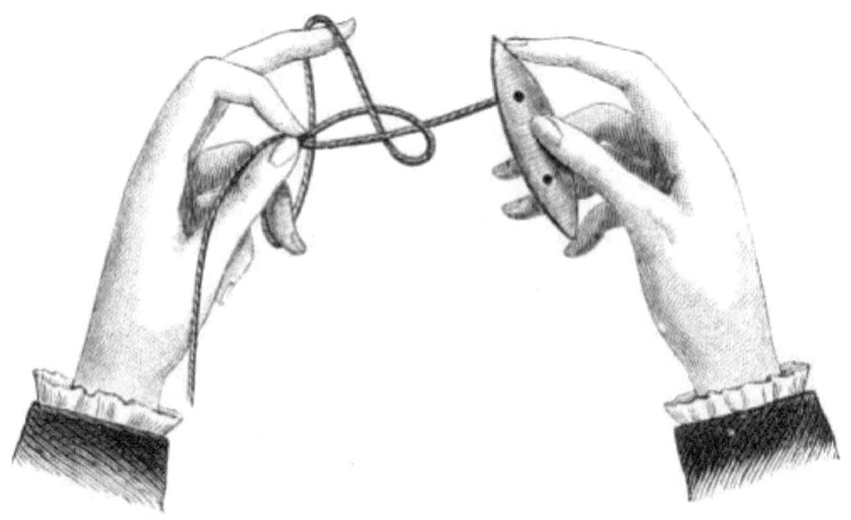

Fig. 488. Third position of the hands.

Then, raising the third and fourth fingers of the left hand with the loop upon them, pull up the loop, stretching the thread tightly in so doing by extending the fingers. By this movement a knot is formed, the first part of the «double knot», which is the most common one in tatting.

Remember that the right hand must be kept perfectly still as long as the left is in motion and that the knot must be formed of the loop thread that is in the left hand.

The right hand, or shuttle thread, must always be free to run through the knots; if it were itself formed into knots it would not have the free play, needed for loosening and tightening the loop on the left hand, as required.

Fourth position of the hands (fig. 489).—The second part of a knot is formed by the following movements: pass the shuttle, as indicated in fig. 489, from left to right, between the first and third fingers through the extended loop; the right hand seizes the shuttle in front of the empty loop and extends the thread; the left hand pulls up this second part of the knot as it did the first.

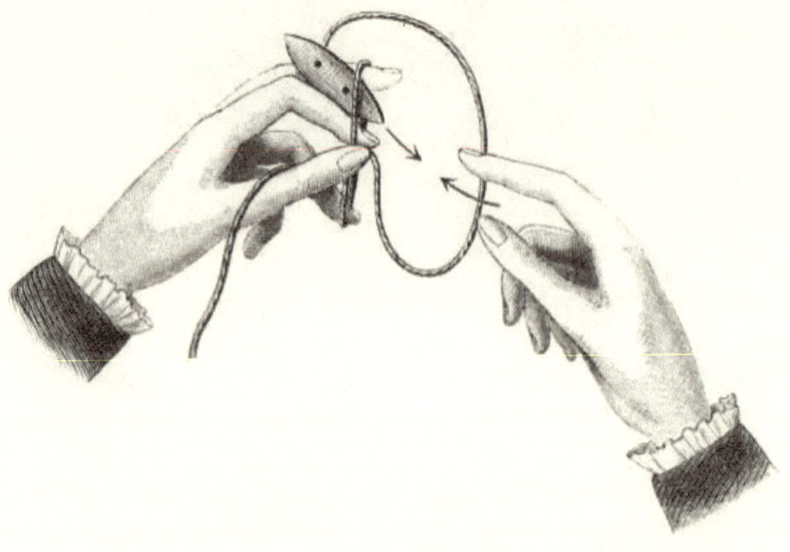

Fig. 489. Fourth position of the hands.

Single or half knots. Josephine picots (figs. 490 and 491).—The Josephine picot or purl, as it is also called in tatting, consists of a series of single or half knots formed of the first knot only. These picots may be made of 4 or 5 knots, as in fig. 490, or of 10 or 12 knots, as in fig. 491.

Fig. 490. Single or half knots. Small josephine picot.

Fig. 491. Single or half knots. Large josephine picot.
Fifth position of the hands (fig. 492).—When the second knot forming the double knot has been made, the two hands resume the position shown in fig. 487. Fig. 492 reproduces the same and shows us a few finished knots as well.

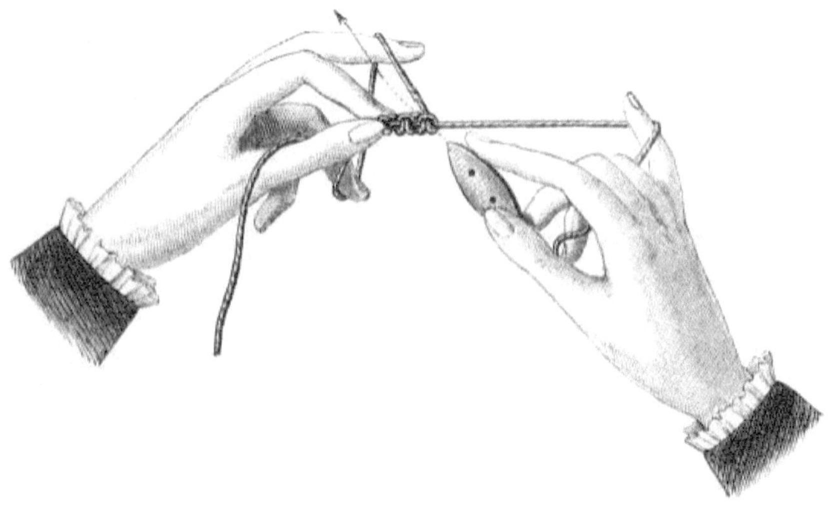

Fig. 492. Fifth position of the hands.
Position of the hands for making a picot (fig. 493).—Picots are introduced into tatting patterns as they are into knitting and crochet. They also serve to connect the different parts of a pattern together and render a great many pretty combinations feasible.

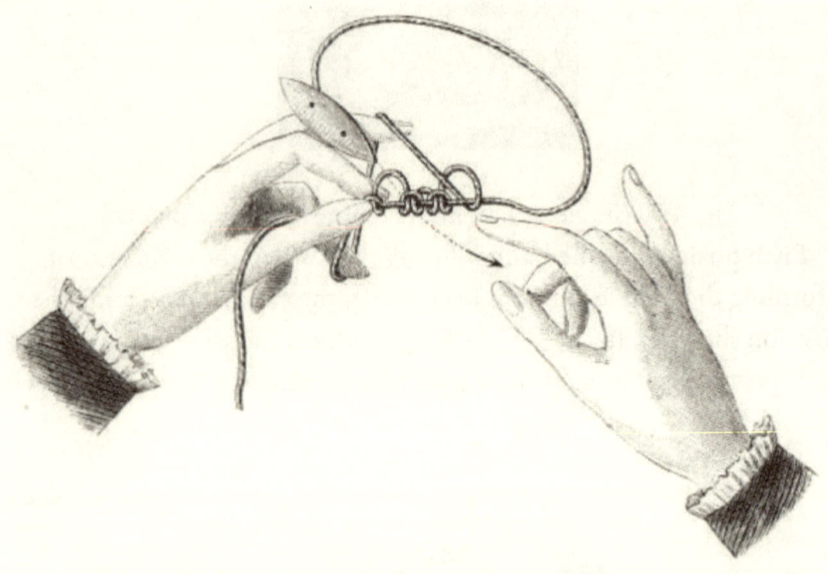

Fig. 493. Position of the hands for making a picot.

Open and close picot (figs. 494 and 495).—These are formed of single knots, leaving a loop on the extended thread, as shown in fig. 494, and a short length of thread between the knots; finish the second half knot and when you have pulled it up, join it to the preceding knot. In this manner the picot represented in fig. 495 is formed quite naturally.

Fig. 494. Open picot.

Fig. 495. Close picot.

In every kind of tatting the knot that comes after the picot is independent of the loop.

Thus if the directions say: 2 knots, 1 picot, 3 knots, 1 picot, 2 knots, etc., you must count the knot that served to form the loop and not make: 2 knots, 1 picot, 4 knots, etc. To join the different rings, ovals, etc., together by means of picots, take up the thread that runs over the left hand with a crochet needle, inserting it into the picot downwards from above, draw the thread through and pull it up like any other knot.

Tatting with two shuttles (fig. 496).—Two shuttles are used in tatting when the little rings are not to be connected together at the bottom by a thread, when you want to hide the passage of the thread to another group of knots and when threads of several colours are used.

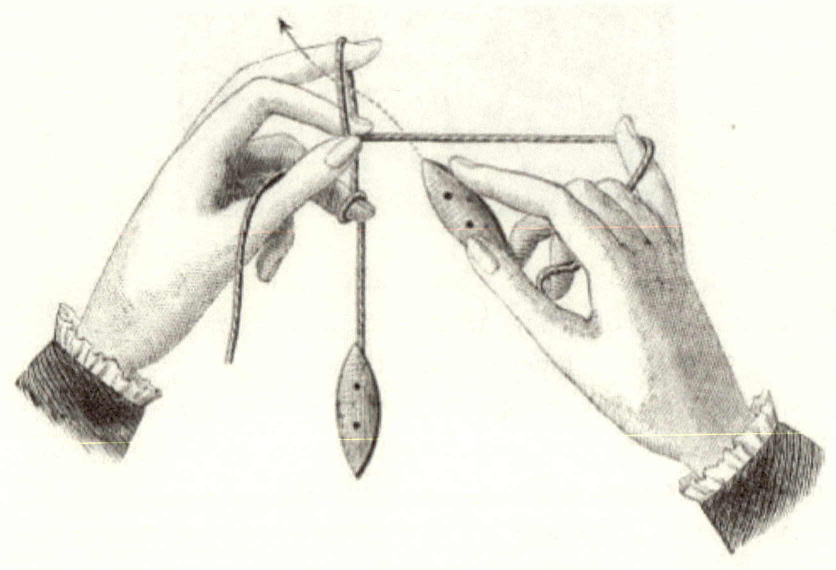

Fig. 496. Tatting with two shuttles.

When you work with two shuttles, tie the two threads together. Pass one thread over the third finger of the left hand, wind it twice round the fourth finger and leave the shuttle hanging down.

Pass the second shuttle into the right hand and make the same movements with it as you do in working with one shuttle only.

Detached scallops (fig. 497).—Make 12 double knots with one shuttle, then tighten the thread so as to draw them together into a half ring; the next knot must touch the last knot of the scallop before it.

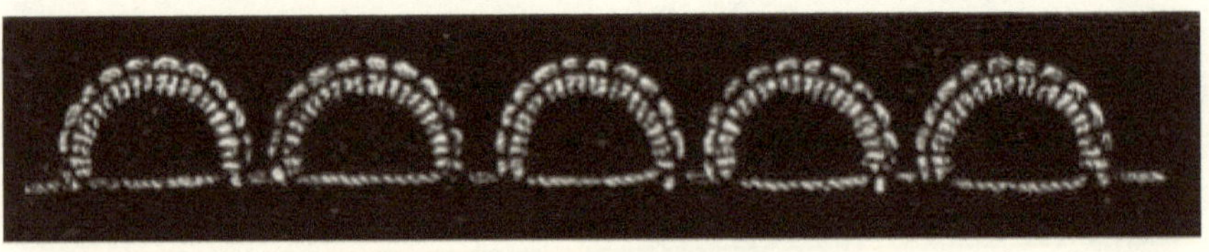

Fig. 497. Detached scallops.

Materials: Fil d'Alsace D.M.C in balls Nos 30 to 70 or Cordonnet 6 fils D.M.C Nos. 25 to 50.[A]

Scallops joined together at the top (fig. 498). With one shuttle make 4 double, 1 picot, * 8 double, 1 picot, 4 double, close the half ring, 4 double, draw the thread through the picot and repeat from *.

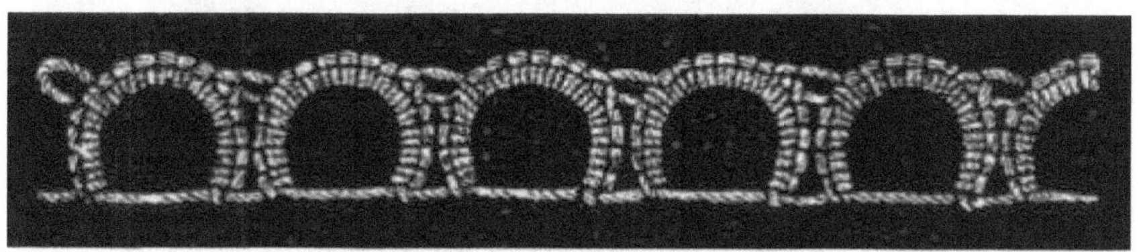

Fig. 498. Scallops joined together at the top.

Materials: Fil d'Alsace D.M.C Nos. 30 to 70, Cordonnet 6 fils D.M.C Nos. 15 to 40, or Fil à dentelle D.M.C Nos. 25 to 60 [A]

Scallops with picots (fig. 499).—Make with one shuttle: 4 double, 1 picot, * 3 double, 1 picot, 2 double, 1 picot, 2 double, 1 picot, 3 double, 1 picot, 4 double, close the ring.

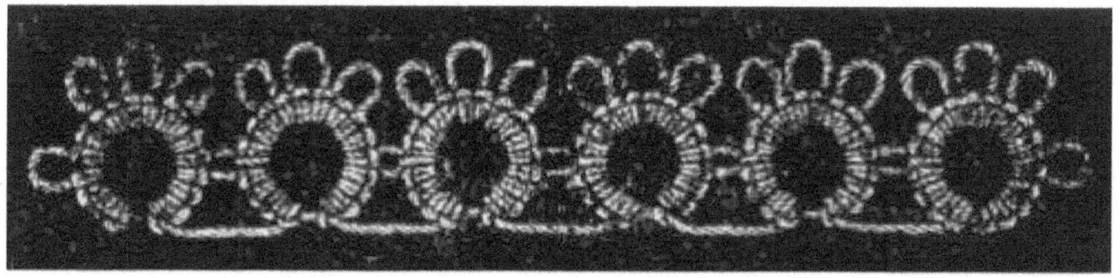

Fig. 499. Scallops with picots.

Materials: Fil d'Alsace D.M.C in balls Nos. 30 to 70, écru or white.[A]

Leave sufficient length of thread before beginning the next ring, for the rings not to overlap each other = make 4 double, draw the left hand thread through the 5th picot of the preceding ring and repeat from *.

Tatted insertion (fig. 500).—Make with one shuttle a ring like the ones in fig. 499, then leaving a length of, from 5 to 10 m/m. of thread, make a second ring = turn the work = leave the same length of thread again, begin a third ring which you join after the 4th double, to the 5th picot of the 1st ring = turn the work after each ring is made, so that all the upper rings represent the right side of the work and all the lower ones the wrong.

Fig. 500. Tatted insertion.
Materials: Fil d'Alsace D.M.C in balls Nos. 30 to 70, écru or white.

Tatted insertion (fig. 501).—To be worked with two shuttles. Begin with one thread and one shuttle and make a ring, as in figs. 499 and 500; and a second close to it; then pass the thread over the left hand, take the second shuttle in the right hand and make 6 double on the 2nd thread, after which you again make a ring above and one below with one shuttle only.

Fig. 501. Tatted insertion.
Materials: Fil d'Alsace D.M.C Nos. 30 to 70, or Cordonnet 6 fils
D.M.C No. 20.

Edging of tatting and crochet (fig. 502).—Make with one shuttle: 1 double, 1 picot, 2 double, 1 picot, 2 double, 1 picot, 2 double, 1 picot twice as long as the others, 2 double, 1 picot, 2 double, 1 picot, 2 double, 1 picot, 2 double, 1 long picot, 1 double = close the ring = fasten off the two threads on the wrong side with two or three stitches.

Fig. 502. Edging of tatting and crochet.
Materials—For the tatting: Fil d'Alsace D.M.C in balls No. 30. For the crochet: Cordonnet 6 fils D.M.C No. 60.

After the first knot join the next ring to the preceding one by the long picot, and work the remainder as has been already described.

When you have a sufficient number of rings, pick up the picots by crochet trebles with 3 chain stitches between them. On this first row, crochet a second, consisting of: 2 chain, 1 picot, 2 chain, 1 single in the treble of the 1st row. To finish the bottom part of the work, make 1 plain in the 1st picot, 3 chain; 1 plain in the 2nd picot, 3 chain, 1 plain in the 3rd picot, 1 chain, 1 plain in the 1st picot of the next ring.

One row of single crochet serves as a footing to the edging.

Tatted edging in three rows (fig. 503).—Worked with two shuttles. The first row is worked like fig. 495, with one shuttle. The second and third are worked with two.

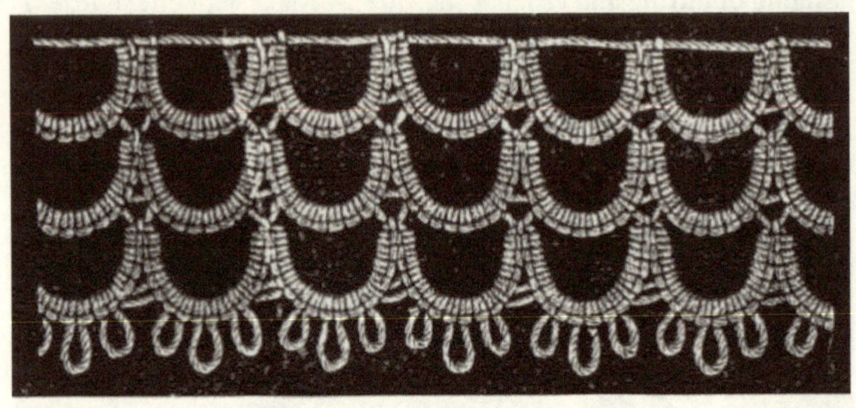

Fig. 503. Tatted edging in three rows.
Materials: Fil d'Alsace D.M.C in balls Nos. 30 to 70, or Cordonnet 6 fils D.M.C Nos. 20 to 60.

Fasten the thread of the right hand shuttle into the first picot; then work on this thread the same number of double knots and picots as in the 1st row and join each half ring to the picot of the row before. In the 3rd row, insert 3 picots between the 8 double knots of the row above. Here the Josephine picot may be substituted for the plain picot.

Tatted edging (fig. 504).—Worked with two shuttles and two colours. After making a string of rings like those in fig. 502, with Fil d'Alsace D.M.C No. 30 écru, fasten the blue and unbleached threads of the respective shuttles to the middle picot. Holding the light thread in the right hand, and the dark one laid over the left hand, work: 3 double, 1 picot, 3 double = then put the right hand thread separately through the 2 picots of the rings and continue to make: 3 double, 1 picot, 3 double.

Fig. 504. Tatted edging.
Materials: Fil d'Alsace D.M.C in balls Nos. 30 to 70, or Fil à dentelle
D.M.C Nos. 25 to 50.
Colours: Écru and Bleu-Indigo 334, or Jaune d'Ocre 667 and
Rouge-Cornouille 450, Gris-Tilleul 331 and Brun-Caroubier 356.
The next row also is made with two shuttles. Hold the light thread in
the right hand; with the dark thread, laid across the left hand, make: *
4 double, 1 picot, 2 double, 1 picot, 2 double = turn the work = with
the right hand shuttle make: 6 double, put the thread through the
little picot formed above the middle picot of the rings, 6 double, close
the ring = turn the work = make with two shuttles: 2 double, 1 picot,
2 double, 1 picot, 4 double, put the light thread through the 2 blue
picots and repeat from *. The first row of crochet for the footing
consists of chain and plain stitches only, the second, of chain stitches
and trebles.

Medallion (fig. 505).—Take two colours of thread and fill two
shuttles with the light colour and two with the dark. Make with one
shuttle: 24 double and 12 picots, 6 of them short and 6 long; close the
ring, break off the thread and fasten off the ends by a stitch or two on
the wrong side.—For the next 4 rows take two shuttles.

Fig. 505. Medallion.
Materials: Fil d'Alsace D.M.C in balls Nos. 30 to 50.[A]
Colours: White and Rouge-Géranium 352, or écru and Vert-Mousse
471, Bleu pâle 668 and Jaune d'Or 676.

1st row—with the shuttles containing the light colour = fasten the
ends on to a short picot and make: * 3 double, 1 short picot, 2 double,
1 long picot, 2 double, 1 long picot, 2 double, 1 long picot, 2 double, 1
short picot, 3 double; pass the right hand thread through one of the
short picots of the first ring, repeat the series 5 times from *.
When you reach the 6th half ring, instead of making the second picot,
put the left hand thread through the short picot of the first half ring,

then complete the last double knots, cut the threads off, pass them through the picot of the ring and fasten them off on the wrong side.

2nd row—with the shuttles filled with the light colour = fasten the ends on to a long picot, then make: * 4 double, 1 picot, 4 double, pass the right hand thread through the picot of the first row and repeat the series 17 times from *.

3rd row—with the shuttles filled with the dark colour = fasten the ends on to one of the picots of the last row and make: * 4 double, pass the right hand thread through the picot of the 2nd row, make a long picot, 4 double and repeat this series all round the medallion, until you have 18 scallops.

4th row—with the shuttles filled with the dark colour = * 2 double, 1 picot, 2 double, 1 picot, 2 double, 1 picot, 2 double, pass the right hand thread, from the wrong side, through the picot of the 2nd row and begin again from *.

Insertion of tatting and crochet (fig. 506).—Fill two shuttles, one with a light colour, say, Bleu de France 344, the other with a darker, such as Jaune-Rouille 365, and two numbers coarser than the thread you intend to use for the crochet. Begin with the dark colour and make: * 4 double, 1 picot, 8 double, 1 picot, 4 double, close the ring. With both shuttles, the light colour in the left hand: 4 double, 1 picot, 2 double, 1 picot, 2 double, 1 picot, 4 double, put the right hand thread through the picot of the first circle; then add: 4 double, 1 picot, 2 double, 1 picot, 2 double, 1 picot, 4 double.

Fig. 506. Insertion of tatting and crochet.
Materials: Fil d'Alsace D.M.C in balls Nos. 30 to 70, or Fil à dentelle
D.M.C Nos. 25 to 50.
Colours: Bleu de France 344 and Jaune-Rouille 365.

With the shuttle, filled with the dark colour: 5 double, pass the thread
through the picot of the first ring, make 8 double, 1 picot, 5 double,
close the ring. Then, leaving a short length of thread between, make: 4
double, put the thread through the picot of the preceding ring, 8
double, 1 picot, 4 double, close the ring **; then repeat from * to **.
When you have thus made two equal lengths, join them together with
crochet, using a thread two numbers finer than the tatting thread; if
the latter for instance was Fil d'Alsace No. 30, you would take No. 50
of the same material for the crochet—1 plain in the 1st picot, 5 chain,
1 plain in the middle picot, 5 chain, 1 plain in the 3rd and 1st picot =
then, over 5 chain: 1 sextuple cluster stitch (fig. 426), 5 chain.
In the row on the opposite side of the tatting, take out the crochet
needle at the 3rd chain stitch and put it in from beneath into the

corresponding stitch of the opposite row; in this manner join the two insertions together so as to complete the pattern.

Insertion of tatting and crochet (figs. 507 and 508).—Worked with one shuttle. The tatting thread should be two numbers coarser than the crochet thread. Begin with 2 strings of half rings consisting of: 4 short picots and 3 long. Leave a length of thread between, equal to the diameter of the ring.

Fig. 507. Insertion of tatting and crochet.
Materials—For the tatting: Fil d'Alsace D.M.C in balls Nos. 30 to 70, or Cordonnet 6 fils D.M.C Nos. 25 to 50, écru or white.[A]
For the crochet: The same materials, but two numbers finer.
When the two strings of half rings are finished, crochet with the fine thread: 6 plain over each length of thread between, and at the base of the scallops.

Fig. 508. Working detail of fig. 507.

2nd row—5 chain, 1 plain in the 4th plain of the 1st row.
In the row that connects the two rows of tatting, put the 3rd chain stitch into the corresponding stitch of the opposite row.

For the outside edge make: 1 plain in the 1st short picot, 8 chain *, 1 treble in the 2nd short picot, 7 chain, 1 treble in the 3rd short picot, 8 chain, 1 plain in the 4th short picot, 1 plain in the short picot opposite, 3 chain, pass the thread through the 4th of the 8 chain stitches, 4 chain and repeat from *.

For the last row make: 3 plain in each of the 3 last of 8 chain, * 1 picot of 5 chain above the treble, 4 plain in the 4 next chain, 1 picot, 1 single in the same stitch as the plain before the picot, 3 plain, 1 picot, 3 plain, miss the 1st and the last stitch, then make 3 plain on the next scallop and repeat from *.

Edging of tatting and crochet (fig. 509).—Worked with two shuttles and in two shades. With the light shade: 2 double, 1 short picot, 2 double, 1 long picot, * 2 double, 1 picot of the ordinary size, 2 double, 1 picot, 2 double, 1 picot, 2 double, 1 long picot, 2 double, 1 short picot, 2 double, close the ring = with 2 shuttles: 3 double, pass the thread through the 1st picot, make 3 double, 1 long picot, 2 double = with the light shade: 4 double, pass the thread through the 9th picot of the 1st ring, make 3 double, 1 picot, 4 double, close the ring = with 2 shuttles: 2 double, 1 picot, 3 double, 1 short picot, 3 double = with one shuttle: 2 double, pass the thread through the empty picot of the small ring, make 2 double, pass the thread through the long picot of the big ring, then repeat from *.

Fig. 509. Edging of tatting and crochet.

Materials—For the tatting: Fil d'Alsace D.M.C in balls No. 30 in two shades of one colour.

For the crochet: Fil d'Alsace D.M.C in balls No. 50 in one colour only.

To complete the edge, crochet first one row, consisting of: * 1 plain in the 1st of the 5 picots of the big ring, 4 chain, 1 plain in the 2nd picot, 4 chain, 1 plain in the 3rd picot, 4 chain, 1 plain in the 4th picot, 4 chain, 1 plain in the 5th picot and repeat from *.

2nd row—2 plain on the 3rd and 4th of the first chain stitches = over the 2nd and 3rd chain: 1 plain, 1 half treble, 2 trebles, 1 half treble, 1 plain; on the 4 last chain: 2 plain.

For the footing make: 1 plain in the long picot, 5 chain, 1 plain in the next picot, 5 chain, 1 double treble in the short picot, leave the 2 last loops of the treble on the needle = 3 trebles in the first lower loop of the double treble, keep the last loops of these 3 trebles on the needle, after the 4th treble, draw the needle through the 4 trebles. The last row consists of: 3 chain, 1 treble over 5 chain.

Tatted medallion (fig. 510).—Worked with two shuttles and two colours.

Fig. 510. Tatted medallion.
Materials: Fil d'Alsace D.M.C Nos. 30 to 50.[A]
Colours: Gris-Tilleul 330 and Rouge-Cardinal 304.[A]
1st row—with one shuttle: 12 double and 6 picots, close the ring.
2nd row—with two shuttles and the dark coloured thread laid across
the left hand = knot the threads into one of the picots of the 1st ring:
1 double, 1 long picot, 2 double, pass the right hand thread through
one of the picots of the ring, 1 picot, 2 double and so on. After the
12th picot fasten off the threads on the wrong side by two or three
stitches.
3rd row—with one shuttle: * 3 double, pass the thread through one of
the picots of the 2nd row, make 3 double, close the ring = leave 5 m/

m. of thread = turn the work = 4 double, 1 picot, 4 double, close the ring = leave 5 m/m. of thread again and repeat 11 times from *.

4th row—with two shuttles; fasten the ends to one of the picots of one of the 12 rings of the 3rd row: * 3 double, 1 picot, 3 double = with one shuttle: 3 double, pass the thread through the picot, 3 double, 1 picot, 2 double, 1 picot, 3 double, close the ring = close to this: 3 double, pass the thread through the 2nd picot of the 1st ring, 3 double, 1 picot, 3 double, close the ring = again, close to the last ring: 3 double, pass the thread through the picot of the 2nd ring, 2 double, 1 picot, 3 double, close the ring = with 2 shuttles: 3 double, pass the thread through the 2nd picot of the 3rd ring, 3 double, fasten the thread to the picot of the ring of the 3rd row and repeat 11 times from *.

5th row—with two shuttles and the dark colour across the left hand: 6 double and 2 picots over the lower rings and 10 double and 4 picots over the upper rings.

Tatted edging (fig. 511).—With two shuttles and with the two colours indicated, or in any other combination of colours.

Fig. 511. Tatted edging.

Materials: Fil d'Alsace D.M.C in balls Nos. 30 to 70, Cordonnet 6 fils
D.M.C Nos. 40 to 50, or Fil à dentelle D.M.C Nos. 25 to 40.

Colours: Gris-Tilleul 330 and Rouge-Grenat 326.

Begin with two shuttles, the red thread across the left hand = 10
double, 1 picot, 6 double = with one shuttle: 6 double, 1 picot, 6
double, close the ring = turn the work = make a second ring like the
first and close to it = turn the work = with two shuttles: 6 double, 1
picot, 6 double = with one shuttle: 6 double, pass the thread through
the picot of the ring opposite, 6 double, close the ring = 6 double, 1
picot, 6 double, close the ring = turn the work to make the next half
ring.

Make 3 rows of half rings connected by rings. In the 2nd row, you pass
the thread from the ring through the picot to which the 2nd ring was
fastened in the 1st row.

For the outside scallops, make with one shuttle: * 5 double, pass the thread through the picot that connects 2 rings, 5 double, close the ring = with two shuttles: 4 double = with one shuttle: 2 double, 1 picot, 2 double, 1 picot, 2 double, pass the thread through the picot of the half ring of the 3rd row, 2 double; then 8 picots more with 2 double between each, close the ring = with two shuttles: 4 double, 1 long picot, 2 double, 1 short picot, 2 double, 1 short picot, 3 double = with one shuttle: 5 double, pass the thread through the 3rd picot of the big ring, 5 double, close the ring = with two shuttles: 2 double, 6 picots with 2 double after each picot = with one shuttle: 5 double, pass the thread through the 3rd picot of the big ring, 5 double, close the ring = with two shuttles: 3 double, 1 picot, 2 double, 1 picot, 2 double, 1 picot, 4 double, pass the right hand thread through the 6th picot of the big ring = with two shuttles: 4 double, then repeat from *.
The footing is worked in crochet and consists of one row of chain stitches and one of trebles.

Square of tatting (fig. 512).—Worked with two shuttles and two colours. With the light colour: 2 double, 1 picot, 4 double, 1 picot, 4 double, 1 picot, 4 double, 1 picot, 2 double, close the ring.

Fig. 512. Square of tatting.

Materials: Fil d'Alsace D.M.C in balls Nos. 30 to 100, Cordonnet 6 fils
D.M.C Nos. 10 to 60, or Fil à dentelle D.M.C Nos. 25 to 70. [A]
Colours: Jaune-Rouille 366 and Brun-Caroubier 359.[A]

1st row—with two shuttles, the dark coloured thread across the left
hand = fasten the thread to a picot and make: * 2 double, 1 picot, 2
double, 1 picot, 2 double, 1 picot, 2 double, pass the right hand thread
through the picot of the ring; 1 picot over the connecting thread, then
repeat 3 times from *. The last picot over the picot of the small ring is
made at the end.

2nd row—with two shuttles, the light thread over the left hand =
fasten the thread to the picot over the light picot: * 2 double, pass the

right hand thread through the picot of the 1st row, 1 long picot over the lower picot, 3 double, pass the thread through the next picot of the 1st row = in the corner, 1 rather longer picot than the one before, 3 double, pass the right hand thread through a picot, 1 long picot, 2 double, pass the thread through a picot; repeat 3 times from *. To form the last picot, fasten off the thread on the wrong side by two or three stitches.

3rd row—with one shuttle and the dark colour: * 4 double, pass the thread through the picot above the picot of the small ring, 4 double, close the ring = leave 10 m/m. of thread, make a second ring like the 1st = leave 10 m/m. of thread, make 6 double, pass the thread through the long picot, 6 double, close the ring = leave 10 m/m. of thread, make another ring of 12 knots, fasten it to the same picot, the preceding knot is fastened to; then make a ring of 8 double knots and repeat 3 times from *.

4th row—with one shuttle and the light colour and worked like the 3rd row, leaving a rather longer length of thread between; then make: 16 instead of 12 double for the corner rings.

5th row—with one shuttle and the light colour = 8 double, fasten the thread to one of the corner loops and between 2 rings of the 4th ring: 8 double, close the ring = turn the work = leave a length of thread, 3 double, 1 picot, then 4 times 2 double knots and 1 picot, 3 double, close the ring. Make the second ring as close as possible to the first, beginning and finishing the second with 5 double knots = make a 3rd ring like the 1st, join it to the 2nd ring by the 4th picot = turn the work = make another ring of 16 knots and join it to the same loop of the 4th row, to which the two other rings are already joined = turn the work = 1 ring above, with 4 picots, like the first one we described, then a ring of 12 double knots below.

At the top, 6 detached half rings, placed between 3 connected rings, which form the corners. The top rings are to be joined after the 3rd double knot, to the 4th picot of the preceding ring.

6th row—with two shuttles and the dark colour only = fasten the threads to a picot that serves as a connecting link, take the dark thread over the left hand and make: 3 double, 1 picot, 2 double, 1 picot, 2 double, 1 picot, 3 double = fasten the thread to the connecting picot and carry the half rings all-round the square.

TATTING PATTERNS.

1.—Pine Pattern Collar in Tatting.

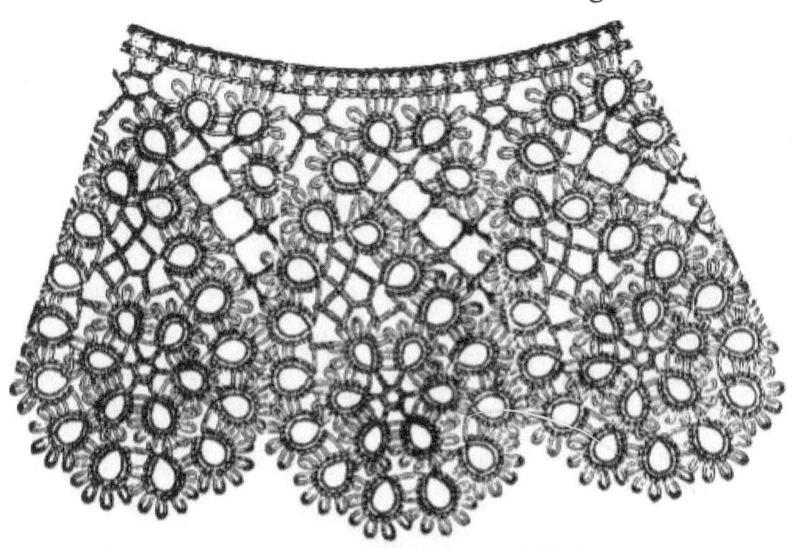

1.—Pine Pattern Collar in Tatting.

Materials: Messrs. Walter Evans and Co.'s Boar's Head cotton No. 80, or tatting cotton No. 60; tatting-pin No. 3; a small shuttle.

This collar is worked with very fine tatting cotton as follows:—*1st circle:* 2 double, 1 purl 7 times, 2 double, draw up the cotton.

2nd circle: 3 double, join it to the last purl of the 1st circle, 1 double, 1 purl 8 times, 2 double, draw the cotton up.

3rd circle: 2 double, join it to the last purl of the 2nd circle, 1 double, join it to the 7th purl of the 2nd circle, 1 double, 1 purl 8 times, 2 double, draw the cotton up.

4th circle: 2 double, join it to the last purl of 3rd circle, 3 double, 1 purl, 1 double 7 times, 1 double, draw the cotton up.

5th circle: 2 double, join it to the last purl of 4th circle, 2 double, 1 purl, 1 double 3 times, draw up the cotton.

6th circle: 2 double, join it to the last purl of the 5th circle, 1 double, join it to the 5th purl of the preceding circle, 1 double, 1 purl 6 times, 1 double, join it to the first purl of the 1st circle, 2 double, draw up the cotton. This completes the star pattern in centre of pine.

1st circle of pine: 2 double, 1 purl, 1 double 8 times, 2 double, draw up the cotton.

2nd circle: 3 double, join to the last purl of 1st circle, 1 double, join it to the 7th purl of 1st circle, 1 double, 1 purl 6 times, 3 double, draw up the cotton and join it to the 3rd purl of centre star.

3rd circle: 3 double, join to the last purl of 2nd circle, 1 double, 1 purl 8 times, 2 double, draw up the cotton and join it on to the centre purl of 2nd circle in star.

4th circle: 2 double, join to the last purl of 3rd circle, 1 double, 1 purl 5 times, 3 double, 1 purl, 2 double, draw up the cotton and join it to the 5th purl of 2nd centre circle in star.

5th circle: 2 double, join the cotton to the last purl of 4th circle, 1 double, 1 purl 7 times, 2 double, draw up the cotton, repeat the 5th circle twice more, then join the cotton to the centre purl of 4th circle in star.

8th circle: 2 double, join to the last purl of 7th circle, 1 purl, 1 double 5 times, 2 double, draw up the cotton and join it to the centre purl of 5th circle in star.

9th circle: 2 double, join to the last purl of 8th circle, 1 double, 1 purl 6 times, 2 double, draw up the cotton. Repeat the 9th circle 3 times.

13th circle: 3 double, join the cotton to the last purl of the 12th circle, 1 double, 1 purl 7 times, 4 double, draw up the cotton, turn the work downwards, and work the

14th circle: 2 double, 1 purl, 3 double, join it to the 1st purl of the 1st circle of pine, 1 double, join it to the 2nd purl of first pine circle, 1 double, 1 purl 6 times, 2 double, draw up the cotton.

15th circle: 3 double, join to the last purl of the 13th circle, 1 double, 1 purl 6 times, 3 double, draw up the cotton.

16th circle: 3 double, join to the last purl of the 15th circle, 1 double, 1 purl 4 times, 3 double, 1 purl, 1 double, draw up the cotton.

17th circle: 1 double, join to the last purl of the 16th circle, 1 double, 1 purl 6 times, 2 double, draw up the cotton.

18th circle: 1 double, join to the last purl of the 17th circle, 1 double, 1 purl 8 times, 1 double, draw up the cotton, and repeat from commencement until the collar is the required size. The upper part of the pines is filled in with lace stitches, as clearly shown in our illustration.

2.—*Tatted Insertion.*

Materials: Messrs. Walter Evans and Co.'s tatting cotton No. 30, or Boar's Head crochet cotton No. 12; tatting pin No. 2; large shuttle.

2.—Tatted Insertion.

This insertion should be worked with coarse cotton. 5 double *, 1 purl, 2 double, repeat from * 4 times, 1 purl, 5 double, draw up the cotton, turn the pattern downward, and work another circle the same as that

above described, leaving one-sixth of an inch of cotton between each
circle.

3.—*Lace Edging in Tatting.*

Materials: Messrs. Walter Evans and Co.'s crochet cotton No. 10, or
tatting cotton No. 20; tatting-pin No. 3; any sized shuttle. For a finer
edging, No. 18.

1st oval: Fill the shuttle, but do not cut it off from the reel, as a double
thread is used, and commence by working 10 double stitches, 1 purl,
10 double; draw up.

Double thread: Putting the thread attached to the reel round the left
hand, work 8 double, 1 purl, 8 double.

3.—Lace Edging in Tatting.

2nd oval: 10 double, join to purl in 1st oval, 10 double; draw up.
The pattern is now complete. Repeat from beginning, taking care that
the next oval be close to the last.

Crochet a heading with the same cotton, working 7 chain, 1 double
into the purl in double thread. Repeat.

4.—*Lace Edging in Tatting.*

Materials: Messrs. Walter Evans and Co.'s crochet cotton No. 10, or
tatting cotton No. 20; tatting-pin No. 3; any sized shuttle. For a finer
edging, No. 18.

4.—Lace Edging in Tatting.

1st oval: Fill the shuttle, but do not cut it off from the reel, as a double thread is required, and commence by working 10 double stitches, 1 purl, 10 double stitches, draw up.

2nd oval: Close to last oval, work 10 double, 1 purl, 10 double; draw up.

Double thread: Putting the thread attached to the reel round the left hand, work 12 double, 1 purl, 4 double; then join the shuttle-thread to the purl in 2nd oval, by drawing it through with a pin. Then do another similar chain of stitches with the double thread, viz., 4 double, 1 purl, 12 double.

3rd oval: 10 double, join to the purl in 2nd oval—the same as that to which the shuttle-thread has been fastened—10 double; draw up.

4th oval: Close to last oval, work 10 double, join to purl of 1st oval, 10 double, draw up.

The pattern is now complete. Repeat from beginning, taking care that the next oval be close to the last. Crochet a heading with the same cotton, working 4 chain, 1 double into the purl of double thread, 6 chain, 1 double into the next purl. Repeat.

5.—*Border in Tatting with Crochet Edging.*

Materials: Messrs. Walter Evans and Co.'s tatting cotton No. 60, or crochet cotton No. 80; tatting-pin No. 2; a bone shuttle.

5.—Border in Tatting with Crochet Edging.

Work * 4 double stitches (that is, 4 times following 1 purled stitch and 1 plain), 1 purl, four times following 3 double stitches, 1 purl, 4 double stitches, draw up the cotton so as to form an oval, and for the smaller oval, work 9 double stitches, but leave, before beginning the first double stitch, the space of one-sixth of an inch between this oval and the preceding; repeat from *, leaving the same space between each oval; join together the larger ovals by the purl.

For the crochet edging, work the 1st row in the following manner:—1 double (followed by 6 chain) in each of the smaller ovals. The 2nd and 3rd rows are composed of short treble stitches, placed one above the other, and divided by one chain. While working the short treble stitches of the 3rd row form the small purl thus:—

* 1 short treble in the first short treble of preceding row, let the loop slip off from the crochet needle, insert the needle in the under stitch, from which comes the loop now made into a purl, work 1 double in the first short treble of preceding row, 1 chain, under which miss 1 stitch, and repeat from *.

6.—*Border in Tatting with Crochet.*

Materials: Messrs. Walter Evans and Co.'s Boar's Head cotton No. 20, or tatting cotton No. 40; tatting-pin No. 2. For a coarser size use Boar's Head cotton No. 4, or tatting cotton No. 20.

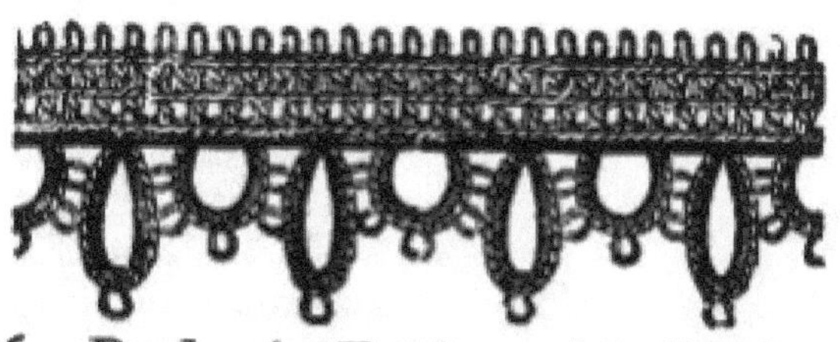

6.—Border in Tatting with Crochet.

4 double stitches, 1 purl, 4 times following, 3 double stitches, 1 purl, 4 double stitches, draw up the oval, but not quite tight, leave a space about one-sixth of an inch, leave a similar space between this oval and the next, work 3 double stitches, fasten them to the nearest purl of preceding oval, then work twice following 4 double stitches, 1 purl, then 3 double stitches, 1 purl, 3 double stitches, and draw up the oval.

7.—*Tatted Insertion.*

Materials: Messrs. Walter Evans and Co.'s Boar's Head crochet cotton No. 18; tatting-pin No. 3.

This strip of insertion is worked with crochet cotton, and consists of a row of circles, two of which are always joined together, and edged on either side with chain stitches. Work first * 2 double, 4 purl divided by 1 double, 1 double, 1 long purl about one-fifth of an inch long, 10 double divided by 1 purl, 1 long purl, 4 times alternately 1 double, 1 purl, then 2 double; join the stitches into a circle; work close to this a second circle, and knot the end of the cotton together with the cotton with which the first circle has been begun; repeat from *, but henceforward in the first of the two circles fasten the cotton on to the middle purl of the preceding circle, instead of working the middle purl. When the strip of insertion is sufficiently long, edge it on either side with a row of chain stitches, by working 1 double in 1 long purl and 5 chain between.

7.—Tatted Insertion.

8.—*Rosette in Tatting.*
Materials: Messrs. Walter Evans and Co.'s tatting cotton No. 40;
tatting-pin No. 3.
This rosette is worked with two cottons, viz., 1 plain, 1 purl, 1 plain, 5
double, 1 purl, 10 double, 1 purl, 1 plain; turn the work downwards,
10 double, fastened on the last purl turned downwards; this forms one
loop turned upwards; turn work downwards, 10 double, 1 purl, 5
double, fastened on first purl turned downwards; turn figure thus
formed downwards; 4 double, 1 single, repeat 4 times more from *,
joining the figures by means of the purl stitch; the ends of the cotton
are knotted together.

8.—Rosette in Tatting.

9.—*Star in Tatting.*
Materials: Messrs. Walter Evans and Co.'s tatting cotton No. 50;
tatting-pin No. 3.

9.—Star in Tatting.

Fill the shuttle, and commencing a loop, work 1 double, then 1 purl and 1 double 12 times, draw into a round; join the cotton to the 1st purl loop. 1st oval.—Commence a loop close to the joining, work 7 double, join to 1st purl of round, work 7 double and draw close; reverse the work. Join the thread from reel, and holding it out for a straight thread, commence the scallop:—
5 double, 1 purl, 5 double, reverse the work. The 2nd oval same as first. Repeat oval and scallop alternately, until the star is completed.

10.—*Insertion worked in Tatting.*
Materials: Messrs. Walter Evans and Co.'s tatting cotton No. 50; tatting-pin No. 3.

10.—Insertion worked in Tatting.

This strip of insertion is worked with two cottons. Work with the cotton in the left hand over that in the right hand. Both ends of cotton are fastened together at the beginning by a knot. First work one half of the insertion the long way in the following manner:—1 plain, 1 purl, 1 plain (the purl must be very short); turn the purl downwards, 6 double, 1 purl, * 6 double, 1 purl, 1 plain, which must all be turned upwards; then turn the work so that the upper edge is turned downwards; work 6 double, fastened on to the last purl turned downwards (the fastening of the stitches is made with the thread in the right hand); a loop turned upwards is thus formed; turn the work downwards, draw the cotton in right hand underneath that in left hand, and work 6 double, 1 purl, 6 double, all turned upwards; fasten these stitches on 1st purl turned downwards. In this pattern 1st of border pattern is thus completed; turn it downwards, 8 double, 1 purl, 8 double, 1 purl, 1 plain, turn work downwards, 6 double, fastened on last purl of last pattern, turned up. Repeat from *. When the insertion is of sufficient length, work the other half in same manner, and fasten it on the 1st half by means of purl stitches between the 8 double stitches twice repeated.

11.—*Tatted Insertion for Trimming Lingeries.*
Materials: Messrs. Walter Evans and Co.'s tatting cotton No. 40, or crochet cotton No. 20; tatting-pin No. 3.

11.—Tatted Insertion.

This insertion consists of 2 rows of three-branched patterns which lie opposite each other, and are joined by slanting rows of knots. A coloured silk ribbon is drawn through these rows which join the patterns. Each of the 3 branches of 1 pattern consists of 9 double, 1 purl, 9 double, and must be worked close to another. When the 3rd branch is completed, fasten another piece of cotton on to the middle branch. Work 12 double over this 2nd piece of cotton, and then work without the 2nd piece of cotton a 2nd three-branched pattern like the 1st.* Fasten the 2nd piece of cotton on to the middle branch of the just-finished pattern, work 12 double over it, then again a three-branched pattern; in this pattern as well as in the following ones, instead of working the purl of the 1st branch, fasten it on to the purl of the 3rd branch of the preceding three-branched pattern of the *same* row, as can be seen in illustration. Repeat till the strip of insertion is sufficiently long.

12.—*Circle in Tatting.*
Materials: Messrs. Walter Evans and Co.'s tatting cotton No. 80;
tatting-pin No. 3.

12.—Circle in Tatting.

Work first 8 ovals, each composed of 5 double stitches, 3 purl divided
one from the other by 4 double stitches, 5 double stitches; these ovals
are joined together by the purl at the sides, then the circle is tightened
as much as possible, and the cotton with which you are working is
twisted round the ends of cotton that have been cut: the cotton is
then fastened off nearly underneath.

Begin a fresh small oval, composed of 12 double stitches, which
should be fastened to the preceding oval after 3 double stitches (to the
purl in the centre of the first oval), then fasten it again to the purl
which joins together the first and the second oval; leave a space of
about one-fourth of an inch, and work an oval composed of 4 double
stitches, 5 purl, followed each by 2 double stitches, 4 double stitches.
A very little farther off make a very small oval, composed of 8 double

stitches, which after the four first double stitches is joined to the centre purl of the second oval, leaving the same space between as before, make another oval of 4 double stitches, 5 purl, each followed by 2 double stitches, 4 double stitches; but the first purl is *missed,* because at this place the oval is joined to the fifth purl of the corresponding oval; once more leave a space of one-fourth of an inch, and repeat. At the end of the round the two ends of cotton are tied tightly together.

13.—*Tatted Border with Beads.*

Materials: Black purse silk, or, for white trimming, Messrs. Walter Evans and Co.'s tatting cotton No. 2; tatting-pin No. 3; 3 hanks of beads No. 4 to the yard of border.

13.—Tatted Border with Beads.

This border, edged with beads No. 4, is worked in middling-size purse silk over fine silk cord of the same colour as the silk. Before beginning to work this pattern, thread the beads which take the place of purl stitches, and which are slipped in between two double stitches. When the row of stitches is of the length required, form the trefoil leaves, and sew a few beads over the places where they are joined. These trefoil leaves are made separately, and then sewn together.

14.—*Insertion in Tatting.*

Materials: Messrs. Walter Evans and Co.'s crochet cotton No. 10;
tatting-pin No. 3; any sized shuttle; for a finer insertion No. 18 or 20.

14.—Insertion in Tatting.

1st oval: Fill the shuttle, but do not cut it off from the reel, as a double thread is used, and commence by working 10 double stitches, 1 purl, 10 double, draw up. Double thread: Putting the thread attached to the reel round the left hand, work 8 double, 1 purl, 8 double.

2nd oval: 10 double, join to purl of 1st oval, 10 double, draw up.

Repeat till the length required is worked, then cut off.

For the fresh length, which will make the other half of the insertion, the shuttle must still be attached to the reel. Commence by working—

1st oval: 10 double, join to the purl which connects the first and second ovals of the piece already worked, 10 double, draw up.

Double thread: 8 double, 1 purl, 8 double.

2nd oval: 10 double, join to the same purl as last—namely, the one connecting the first and second ovals of the piece already worked, 10 double, draw up. Repeat, joining the two next ovals to the purl which connects the two next in the piece already worked, and so on.

Crochet a heading each side, working 7 chain, 1 double into the purl of double thread, repeat. With a heading on one side only, this makes a pretty wide edging.

15.—*Border in Tatting and Crochet.*
Materials: Messrs. Walter Evans and Co.'s tatting cotton No. 40, and crochet cotton No. 80; tatting-pin No. 3.

15.— Border in Tatting and Crochet.

This lace is rendered stronger by the crochet rows of scallops and treble stitch round the edge. Begin with the tatting as follows: Make a circle of 8 double, 7 purl divided by 2 double, 8 double. This circle is repeated at a distance of about three-fourths of an inch, only instead of the 1st purl each following circle must be fastened on to the last purl of the preceding circle. Then take some crochet cotton, which must be finer than the cotton used for tatting, and work a row of double stitches over the thread which joins the circles. The number of stitches depends on the length and size of the cotton; work double stitches round the circles at the place where both ends meet. The outer row consists of treble stitches, which are worked with 1 chain stitch between, missing 1 stitch under each chain. The scallops consist of the two following rows:—1 double, with which the last and first purl of 2 circles are joined, 4 chain; in each of the other purl, 1 double, 4 chain, between 2 double stitches.

2nd row: 1 double in each chain stitch scallop, 1 double, 3 long double, 1 double.

16 and 17.—Lady's Veil in Net and Tatting.

16.—Lady's Veil in Net and Tatting.

This veil is slightly gathered in front and fastened to the brim of the bonnet. It is tied at the back under the chignon. The veil is of black silk net. The flowrets are tatted with black purse silk, and worked in appliqué over the tulle. The veil is edged round with a tatted lace made with the same silk. For the patterns and lace and instructions, see Nos.

18 and 19. No. 16 shows the way in which the veil is worn upon the bonnet, and No. 17 shows its shape when stretched out.

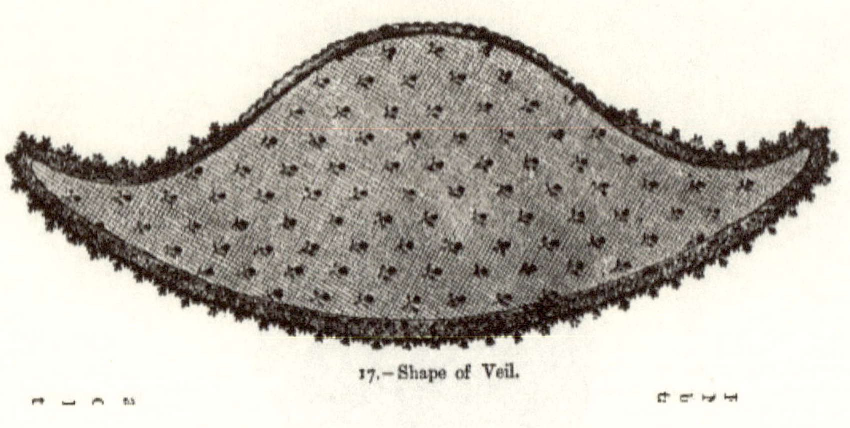

17.—Shape of Veil.

---

18 and 19.—Patterns in Tatting.
Materials: Messrs. Walter Evans and Co.'s tatting cotton No. 120 for a white veil; fine black silk for a black veil; tatting-pin No. 2.

18.—Tatting Pattern for Veil
(16).

19 —Tatting Pattern for Veil
(16).

The patterns Nos. 18 and 19 are meant for ornamenting the veil No. 16. They are sewn upon the net at regular distances.

For working the pattern No. 18, make with black silk or white cotton 6 times alternately 2 double, 1 purl, at the end 1 purl, then join the stitch into a circle, *fasten the silk on to the next purl. Then 1 spot or Josephine knot, consisting of 6 plain stitches, carry the shuttle downwards through the loop, and draw the stitches close together; repeat 3 times more from *. Fasten the silk on to the next purl, and work a circle as follows:—8 times 2 double, divided by 1 purl; fasten the silk on to the next purl, work again 1 spot, after which the silk is fastened, then work 2 more similar circles divided by 1 spot; they are fastened on to the last purl of the preceding circle instead of the 1st purl. Fasten off the silk after the last circle.

For No. 19 work 25 double, divided by 1 purl, join the stitches into a circle, knot the beginning and the end of the cotton together, cut off the ends at a short distance. Then work a smaller circle, consisting of 8 double, divided by 1 purl; at the place of the 1st purl fasten the cotton at a short distance on to the 2nd purl of the large circle. The ends of this circle are knotted together and cut off in the same way. Then work a circle consisting of 11 double, fasten the silk on to the 20th purl of

52

the large circle, work 5 double, and join the stitches into a circle. Then take the ends of the 3 circles, and work close fine stitches with silk round them, so as to form the stem. The completed pattern is sewn upon the net.

---

20 and 21.—Diamond Pattern and Circle in Tatting, for Trimming Linen Collars, Cuffs, &c..
Materials: Messrs. Walter Evans and Co.'s tatting cotton No 30; tatting-pin No. 3.

20.—DIAMOND PATTERN.—

Work, not far one from the other, four leaves, each composed of 5 double stitches, 7 rather long purl divided one from the other by 2 double stitches, 5 double stitches. Instead of making the 1st purl in each of the 3 next leaves, fasten the cotton to the last leaf of preceding leaf. Fasten off and cut the cotton; begin a fresh circle by 2 double stitches, 7 purl divided by 2 double stitches, 2 more double stitches; fasten the cotton to the centre purl of one of the four leaves, and work a very small circle thus:—2 double stitches, fasten the cotton to the last purl of the first circle, 3 double stitches, 1 purl, 2 double stitches; fasten the cotton * to the 6th purl of the leaf; work a larger circle thus:—2 double stitches fastened to the purl of the small circle, 2 double stitches, 4 purl divided by 2 double stitches, 2 more double stitches; fasten the cotton not far off to the second purl of the second leaf; work another small circle similar to that above-described; fasten the cotton to the third purl of the second leaf, then to the fourth purl of the same leaf, and repeat from * three times more, always fastening the first purl of the first circle you are working (each time you repeat the pattern) to the purl of the last small circle last worked; fasten off and cut the cotton.

20.—Diamond in Tatting.

21.—Circle in Tatting.

21.—CIRCLE.—

Begin it in the centre by working a circle of 8 purl, rather long, divided one from the other by 2 double stitches. After you have fastened off and cut the cotton, work * one very small circle composed of 3 double stitches, 1 long purl, 3 double stitches; fasten the cotton not far off to the first purl of the circle, and repeat from * 7 times more, at regular distances. Fasten off and cut the cotton, and begin * a fresh circle of 2 double stitches, 7 purl divided each by 2 double stitches, 2 more double stitches; fasten the cotton to the purl of the very small circle, and work, not far off, a circle of 2 double stitches, 2 purl divided by 2 double stitches, 2 more double stitches; fasten the cotton to the purl of the next small circle, and repeat from * 7 times more. Instead of making the first purl of the next large circle, fasten the cotton to the last purl of the small circle.

22.—Border in Tatting and Crochet.
Materials: Messrs. Walter Evans and Co.'s tatting cotton No. 20;
tatting-pin No. 3.

22.—Border in Tatting and Crochet.

Begin this border with one of the smaller circles consisting of * 3
double, 1 purl, 3 double, 1 purl, 3 double; work a large circle at a short
distance, 5 double, 4 times 1 purl divided by 2 double, 5 double; close
to this circle another as follows:—5 double, fastened on to the last
purl of the preceding circle, 5 times 2 double divided by 1 purl, 1 purl,
5 double; a third circle as follows:—5 double fastened on to the last
purl of the preceding circle, 3 times 2 double divided by 1 purl, 1 purl,
5 double; the cotton is fastened a short distance further on to the
second purl of the first worked small circle, which must be turned
downwards; then turn the work so that the three circles which are
joined together are turned downwards. Work another small circle as
follows at the distance of two-fifths of an inch:—4 double, 1 purl, 4
double, leave again an interval of about two-fifths of an inch, and
repeat from * till the lace is long enough; but in working the following
figures, consisting of three circles, the 1st circle must be fastened on to
the last purl of the 3rd circle at the place of the 1st purl. Complete the

tatting with the 2 following rows of crochet:—* 1 slip stitch in the purl of one of the small circles turned upwards, 5 chain, 1 slip stitch in the next purl, 4 chain; repeat from *. In the following row work 1 double in every stitch.

23.—*Insertion in Tatting and Lace Stitch*.
Materials: Messrs. Walter Evans and Co.'s tatting cotton No. 80; tatting-pin No. 3.

23.—Insertion in Tatting and Lace Stitch.

This insertion forms a very pretty standing-up collar when worked with fine cotton and a coloured ribbon drawn through. It consists of 2 rows of 3 branched figures turned opposite one another, which are worked separately and then joined into a row. Work 9 times as follows:—2 double, 1 purl, 2 double, * draw into a circle and * work at a short distance a 2nd circle as follows:—2 double fastened on to the last purl of the 1st circle, 8 times 2 double, 1 purl, 2 double, repeat once more from *, knot together the two ends of the cotton, and fasten them on the wrong side. One figure is thus completed; each following figure is fastened on to the preceding one on the middle purl of a circle (see illustration). When a sufficient number of such figures have been worked, work a 2nd row of them in the same manner, and fasten from illustration each middle circle of one figure on to the corresponding circle of the 1st row. The circles filled with lace stitch are worked when the 2 rows are completed from illustration in the empty places between 4 patterns; work first 3 double, fasten them on to a purl on the side of a leaf turned inside, * 3 double, fasten them on to a purl of the next leaf, repeat 5 times more from *, work 3 double, join the stitches into a circle, but not too close, so that the purls keep their natural position; cut off the cotton, and fasten the two ends on the wrong side. The lace stitch inside of these circles is worked with fine crochet cotton; the pattern may be changed for a single or double wheel.

24.—*Insertion in Tatting.*
Materials: Messrs. Walter Evans and Co.'s tatting cotton No. 30; tatting-pin No. 3.
Begin by working separately a sufficient number of small rosettes, each composed of six ovals of double stitches and purl. These ovals are worked first in a straight row, then they are joined into a circle and united in the centre by button-hole stitches. The rosettes are joined together with fine cotton. The crochet border is then worked on either side in chain stitches and treble crochet, as seen in illustration.

24.—Insertion in Tatting.

25.—*Centre of a Tatted Couvrette.*

Materials: Messrs. Walter Evans and Co.'s tatting cotton No. 20, or
crochet cotton No. 1; tatting-pin No. 2.

This illustration shows the centre of a tatted couvrette in full size, and
measuring 12 inches across. Separate rosettes like the pattern may be
joined together with smaller ones, and form a very pretty couvrette.
The pattern is worked in rounds. Begin the rosette with a circle,
consisting of 4 double, 1 purl, 6 double, 1 purl, 6 double, 1 purl, 4
double. Take up another shuttle, and work over the cotton on it,
fasten the end on the last double of the circle and work over it,
beginning close to the circle, 6 plain, 1 circle like the 1st worked with
the 1st shuttle, and which is fastened on the last purl of the 1st circle
at the place of the 1st purl; 6 plain, and continue to work so
alternately till you have 7 circles divided by 6 plain stitches. Draw up
very tightly the cotton over which you work, so that the circles form a
rosette, which is closed by sewing together the two corresponding purl
of the first and last circle. Both the ends of the cotton over which you

have worked are knotted together. For the 2nd round, fasten the cotton on one shuttle on the middle purl of a circle, work a circle like those of the 1st round, take up the 2nd shuttle, and work on exactly as in the 1st round, only work 8 plain between the circles over the cotton on the 2nd shuttle. The 2nd round consists of 15 circles; the cotton with which you work must be fastened at the required places on the middle purl of a circle of the preceding round. The 3rd and following rounds are worked in the same manner; the number of circles must be such as to keep the couvrette quite flat. In the pattern the 3rd round has 26 circles. Fasten the cotton well after each round.

25.—Centre of a Tatted Couvrette.

26.—*Tatted Lace.*

Materials: Messrs. Walter Evans and Co.'s tatting cotton No. 30;
tatting-pin No. 2.

26.—Tatted Lace.

This very simple lace consists of scallops which look as if they were slightly gathered. It must be worked with tatting cotton. Each scallop consists of 5 plain, 1 purl, 5 plain, then alternately 5 purled stitches, draw up these stitches till the cotton between the 1st and last stitch is two-fifths of an inch long, and work a 2nd similar scallop at a short distance from the 1st. But in the following scallops fasten each to the last purl of the preceding scallop instead of working the 1st purl.

27.—*Tatted Lace.*

Materials: Messrs. Walter Evans and Co.'s tatting cotton No. 50 or 80;
tatting-pin No. 3.

27.—Tatted Lace.

This pretty lace is worked with fine tatting cotton. Work with 2 threads; the knots are worked over the cotton, which is held in the right hand. Work first the outer scallops of the lace.

Fasten both ends of cotton together and make 10 double, divided by 1 purl, turn the work so as to turn the wrong side upwards, fasten the cotton over which you work on to the last purl, go back over the same row, miss 1 purl next to the cotton with which you work, 9 double divided by 1 purl, fastening the cotton over which you work on the next purl of the 1st row after every double stitch. This forms 1 scallop.

* Turn the work downwards (that is, the purl stitch must be turned downwards), make 4 times 2 double, 1 purl, 1 purled stitch: this is the straight row between 2 outer scallops of the lace. Then work a scallop like the preceding one, fastening it from illustration after the first row on the middle one of the 9 outer purl of the preceding scallop, with the cotton over which you work; repeat from * till the lace is long enough, and fasten the cotton. Knot both ends together again, fasten the cotton over which you work on the first purl of the first scallop, make 9 double, 1 short purl, 1 double, turn so that the upper edge of the row is turned downwards, and the scallops upwards, 5 double, fasten the 2 middle purl of the 4 of the next straight row together by

drawing the cotton, with which you are working through the 2nd purl, so as to form a loop, draw the cotton over which you work through this loop and draw up the latter; work 5 double, fasten the cotton over which you work on to the short purl worked after 9 double, turn the work so that the outer scallops of the lace are turned downwards, 10 double, fasten the cotton over which you work on the first purl of the next scallop, repeat from *, and fasten the cotton. After having fastened both ends together again, turn the work the right side upwards and the outer scallops upwards also, fasten the cotton over which you work on to the short purl which is under the first loop; * work 4 times 2 double, 1 purl, 2 double, fasten the cotton over which you work on the purl under the next loop, and repeat from * till the lace is completed.

28.—*Collar in Tatting and Darned Netting.*
Materials: Messrs. Walter Evans and Co.'s tatting cotton No. 40; tatting-pin No. 3; Messrs. Walter Evans and Co.'s French embroidery cotton No. 60; square netting.

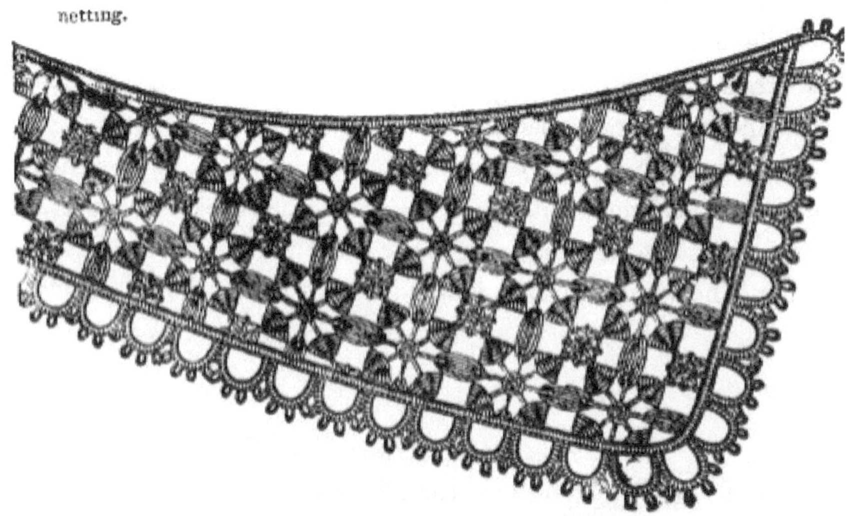

28.—Collar in Tatting and Darned Netting

The pattern is worked with very fine cotton; the netted grounding over a mesh measuring two-fifths of an inch round. The collar is ornamented round the outer edge with a tatted lace. Work a straight strip of netting for the grounding; begin with 2 stitches, work 18 rows backwards and forwards, increasing 1 at the end of each row, so that the last row has 19 holes; work 1 row without increasing; then continue to work with the same number of stitches, increasing 1 at the end of one row and decreasing 1 at the end of the other. When the strip is sufficiently long, work 1 row again without increasing or decreasing, and form the side by making 18 rows, decreasing 1 stitch at the end of each, cast off the 2 last stitches on 1 stitch without forming a new stitch on the needle. Trace the outline of the collar on the grounding with thick cotton, and begin to darn it from illustration. When the darning is completed work the tatted lace with the same cotton, as follows:—6 double, 1 short purl, alternately, 3 times 3 double, 1 purl, 6 double, draw up the stitch so as to form a scallop leaving one-fifth of an inch between the first and last stitch; work a second scallop at a short distance from the first, and so on; every scallop is fastened on to the preceding one after the first 3 double stitches. Work a row of double overcast stitch between the darned netting and the tatted lace; work this row over the cotton tracing, marking the outline of the collar on the grounding and over the cotton between the tatted scallops. Work also a row of double overcast round the neck part, gathering in the collar a little if necessary. Cut away the netting on the wrong side close to the row of overcast stitches.

29.—Mignardise and Tatting.
Materials: Messrs. Walter Evans and Co.'s tatting cotton No. 40; fine mignardise braid.

29.—Mignardise and Tatting.

Patterns formed of mignardise and tatting are of quite new style, and look very pretty. The insertion is easy to work by the following process:—Make first a circle, as follows: 1 plain stitch, 2 double, 1 purl, 6 double, 1 purl, 2 double, 1 plain; fasten the cotton on to one side of the mignardise, at the distance of about five-eighths of an inch, by taking 2 loops of it together; work a second circle at a short distance from the first, and so on. When the strip of insertion is sufficiently long, work in the same manner on the other side of the mignardise. This kind of work is destined to become very popular, and nothing can be more light and graceful than the union of mignardise and tatting.

30.—*Linen Bag for Cotton.*

Materials: Fine linen, 6 inches square; Messrs. Walter Evans and Co.'s tatting cotton No. 40.

30.—Linen Bag for Cotton.

The bag seen in illustration No. 30 is meant to keep the cotton for working a couvrette; it consists of a round piece, measuring 6 inches across, which is hemmed all round, and trimmed with a tatted lace. It is drawn together at top.

31.—*Tatting Insertion.*

Materials: Messrs. Walter Evans and Co.'s cotton No. 30.

The insertion shown in illustration No. 31 is composed in two similar halves. Begin the first in the following way:—10 double, 1 purl, 3 double, 1 purl, 10 double, join the stitches into a circle, and work a second similar circle at a distance of one-third of an inch; instead of the 1st purl, draw the cotton through the 2nd purl of the first-worked circle; leave an interval of one-eighth of an inch, and repeat the two rounds till the insertion is sufficiently long. Then tat round the pieces of cotton which join the two rounds, work round the longest 10 double, and round the shortest 4 double, inserting the shuttle alternately once upwards and once downwards, but for the rest proceeding as in the common button-hole stitch. When the first half is completed, work the second in the same way, and fasten it on to the first with the purl.

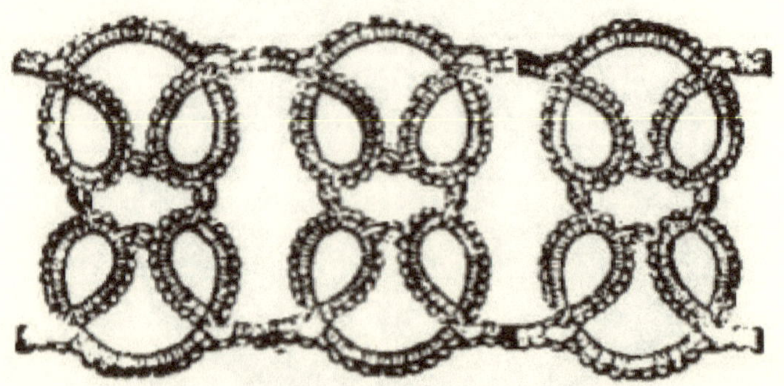

31.—Tatting Insertion.

32.—*Tatting Insertion.*

Materials: Messrs. Walter Evans and Co.'s cotton No. 30.

32.—Tatting Insertion.

The pretty effect of the insertion shown in illustration No. 32 is obtained by means of longer and shorter purl. Work as follows:—Join 9 double into a circle, 1 long purl, 3 double, 1 long purl, 4 double *. After an interval of five-eighths of an inch, begin the large figure of the pattern: 2 double, 1 small purl, 2 double, draw the cotton through the last purl of the small circle, 2 double, drawn through the 1st purl of the same circle, 2 double, 1 small purl, 2 double, 1 long purl, 2 double, 1 small purl, 2 double, repeat 6 times more from *, and draw up. After an interval of five-eighths of an inch comes another small circle: 4 double, draw the cotton through the last purl of the large figure, 3 double, draw the cotton through the next long purl of the same figure, 2 double, 1 long purl, 3 double, 1 long purl, 4 double. Repeat the pattern for the length of insertion required. The threads which join the small circles are worked over with 7 double in the manner described above, only the cotton at the principal figure must be left loose the width of a straw, so as to imitate a long purl. Complete the insertion from illustration by tatting round the small circles of 16 double on the other side (but in the contrary direction), form no purl, but draw the cotton through the long purl of the large figure; the threads which join the 2 circles are likewise drawn through the middle long purl of the large figure; this thread is then tatted over with 7 double, like the opposite outer edge.

33.—*Tatted Square or Diamond.*

Materials: If for couvrettes, Messrs. Walter Evans and Co.'s tatting cotton No. 20, or crochet cotton No. 4; tatting-pin No. 3. For d'oyleys, tatting cotton No. 50; tatting-pin No. 2. For headdresses, tatting cotton No. 80; tatting-pin No. 2.

The square is composed first of nine 4-branched patterns, worked in 3 rows of 3 patterns each, and joined on one to the other with purl. Each pattern consists of 4 branches close to each other, and each branch consists of 7 double, 1 purl, 7 double; when the 4 branches of one pattern are completed, cut off the cotton, and fasten both ends together so as to form a small circle in the centre. Then work a second pattern, which is fastened on to the first and second branches of the first pattern, instead of working the purl stitch; work a third pattern, which is fastened in the same manner on to the second pattern. Then work 2 more rows exactly the same as can be seen in illustration.

33.—Tatted Square.

*For the border of the square, fasten the cotton on the first purl of the first pattern, work 4 double, 13 purl divided by 2 double, 4 double, draw up the stitches close, fasten the cotton again on to the same purl of the first pattern *, and work the following scallop at a short distance:—4 double fastened on the last purl of the preceding circle, 10 purl divided by 2 double, 4 double, draw up the stitch, leaving an interval of two-fifths of an inch between the first and the last; fasten the cotton on to the next purl which joins two patterns, repeat twice more from *, and continue to repeat from *.

34.—*Tatted Rosette.*

Materials: Messrs. Walter Evans and Co.'s tatting cotton No. 40, or crochet cotton No. 60.

34.—Tatted Rosette.

This rosette is very pretty for trimming *lingeries*; it is worked with very fine crochet or tatting cotton. Begin in the centre and work one circle: 16 times alternately 2 double, 1 purl, then 1 purled stitch. Fasten the cotton on to the first purl and work the 2nd round: 1 small circle, consisting of 6 double divided by 1 purl. Fasten the cotton on to the next purl of the middle circle, and repeat in rounds. 3rd round: Fasten the cotton on the middle purl of the first circle of the preceding round, * work at a short distance 8 double divided by 1 purl, join the stitches into a circle, fasten the cotton at the same distance on to the middle purl of the next circle of the preceding round, and repeat in rounds from *, after which the cotton is fastened off.

35.—Rosette in Tatting.

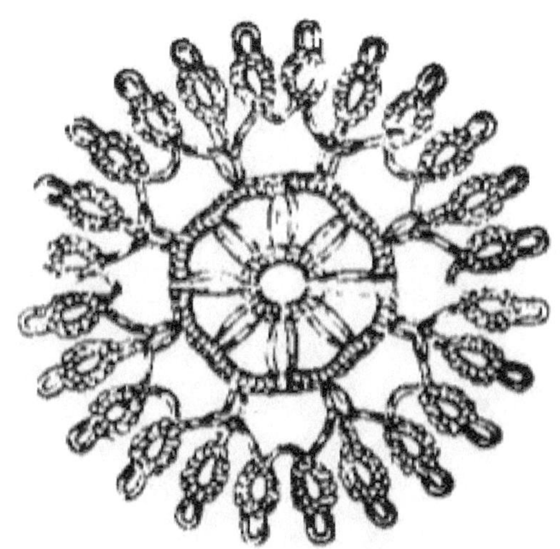

35.—Rosette in Tatting.

Materials: Messrs. Walter Evans and Co.'s tatting cotton No. 40; tatting-pin No. 3.

Begin this rosette with the circle in the centre, and work 8 times alternately 2 double, 1 purl, 1 double, join the stitches into a circle and fasten the cotton. Take a second shuttle and work over the cotton on this shuttle; knot the two ends of cotton together * and work 5 plain, fasten the cotton over which you work on a purl of the circle which is completed, and which must be turned downwards; 5 plain, 1 purl; repeat 7 times more from *, and fasten the cotton. Work now with one of the shuttles the small circles on the outside; * fasten the cotton on to a purl of the second round, and work a circle as follows:—6 double, 1 purl, 6 double, fasten the cotton on to the same purl of the second round, work a similar circle at a short distance, and a third at the same distance. Repeat 7 times more from *, and fasten off the cotton neatly.

36.—Diamond in Tatting.

Materials:Messrs. Walter Evans and Co.'s tatting cotton No. 40;
tatting-pin No. 2.

36.—Diamond in Tatting.

This diamond is suitable for trimming collars, cuffs, &c., when worked
with fine cotton. Work first the four corner patterns separately, as
follows:—7 double, 3 purl divided by 3 double, 6 double, join the
stitches into a circle, work close to this circle a second one consisting
of 6 double fastened on the last purl of the 1st circle, 4 double, 2 purl
divided by 4 double, 6 double; then a 3rd circle consisting of 6 double
fastened on the last purl of the preceding circle, 3 double, 2 purl
divided by 3 double, 7 double. Take a second shuttle, fasten the cotton
on the end of the cotton of the 1st circle, throw the cotton of the 1st
shuttle over the fingers of the left hand, and work with this cotton
over the cotton on the other shuttle in the right hand. Work 5 double,
and then one circle as follows with the cotton in the left hand
only:—8 double fastened on the last purl of the 3rd of the 3 circles
worked close to each other, 5 double, 1 purl, 5 double, 1 purl, 4
double, 1 purl, 6 double, then again over the cotton on the other
shuttle, 5 double, 4 purl divided by 5 double, 5 double, then with one

shuttle only one circle as follows:—6 double, 1 purl, 4 double, 1 purl, 5 double, 1 purl, 5 double fastened on 1st purl of the circle worked at the beginning, 8 double; then again with two shuttles 5 double. Fasten the cotton on the piece of cotton before the 5 double worked with two shuttles, so that the stitches worked over two shuttles form a circle, and cut off the cotton. When three of these patterns have been worked, work the centre pattern of the square. It consists of 4 leaves touching each other at the lower points; each leaf is formed of 3 double, 5 purl divided by 3 double, 3 double; each following leaf is fastened on to the preceding one at the place of the 1st purl. Then work first 1 round of the oval circles of the square, with which the corner patterns are joined. Fasten the cotton on one purl of one corner pattern, make 7 double, 1 purl, 8 double; fasten on the corresponding purl of another corner pattern, work 8 double, 1 purl, 7 double, join the stitches into a circle, fasten the cotton on to the same purl to which the cotton has already been fastened, carry the latter on to the next purl of the same corner pattern, fasten it, then work three more circles like the first, which are fastened on to each preceding circle, at the place of the first purl; fasten the cotton on the two cross purl of the centre pattern, and work four similar circles on the other side of the same. The 8 circles which go across the square in the opposite direction are worked in the same manner. When the square is completed, draw two threads on each side of each corner pattern on to the other side of the square along the cotton which joins the circles together.

37.—Tatting for Cap Crown.
Materials: Messrs. Walter Evans and Co.'s tatting cotton No. 100; tatting-pin No. 1.

37.—Tatting for Cap Crown.

This pattern is very pretty for the crown of a cap, and also for covers, toilet cushions, &c. The size of the cotton depends upon the use you wish to make of the pattern. The pattern is worked with fine tatting cotton. It consists of eight-branched rosettes joined together with small circles. Each rosette is worked as follows: Work 8 loops or branches close to each other, consisting of 7 double, 1 purl, 7 double; fasten both ends of the cotton together, and cut them off. Each of the small circles which joins the rosettes together consists of 2 double, 8 purl divided by 2 double. It is easy to see from the illustration how the patterns are joined together by means of the purl stitches.

---

38 and 39.—Cap in Tatting.
Materials: Messrs. Walter Evans and Co.'s tatting cotton No. 100 tatting-pin No. 1.

38.—Cap in Tatting.

This very pretty cap consists of an oval crown in tatting, edged all round with a tatted lace, the lappets are made in tatting also. The cap is trimmed with large and small rosettes of narrow blue velvet. A narrow velvet ribbon is drawn through the straight open-work edge of the lace, as can be seen in illustration.

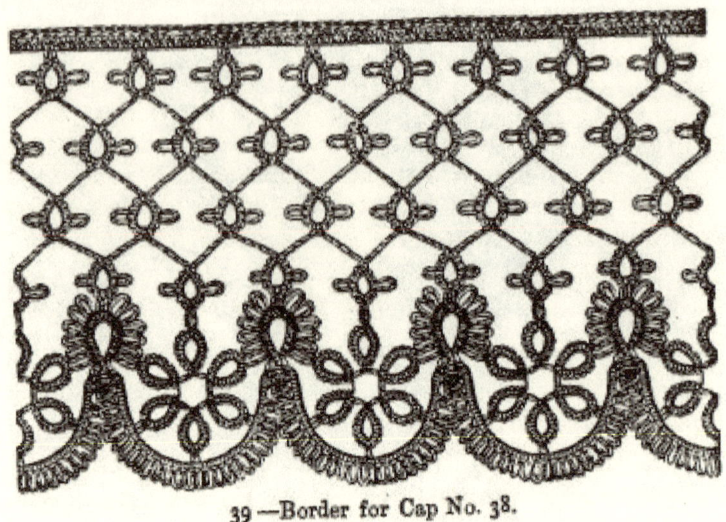

39 —Border for Cap No. 38.

No. 39.—Border for Cap.—The upper part of the border consists of 4 rows of circles worked at a distance of three-fifths of an inch from each other. The circles of the 1st row consist of 3 double, 3 purl divided by 3 double, 3 double. In the following 3 rows each circle is fastened on to the cotton, which joins 2 circles in the 1st row, instead of working the middle purl, the cotton between 2 circles in the last row must only be two-fifths of an inch long. Then work a certain number of six-branched rosettes, each branch consisting of 9 double, 1 purl, 9 double. Each rosette is fastened on to every other circle of the 1st row, as can be seen in illustration. The border is completed as follows:—* 1 double, 6 purl divided by 1 double, 1 purled stitch fastened on to the middle purl of a circle of the 1st row, 1 plain, 6 purl divided by 1 double, join the stitch into a circle, turn the lace so that the rosettes are turned upwards, fasten the cotton on to the purl of the next branch of the next rosette, work 1 double, 7 purl divided by 1 double, 1 double; fasten the cotton on to the purl of the next branch, * work 1 double, 8 purl divided by 1 double, 1 double; fasten the cotton on to the next branch, repeat once more from *, work 1 double, 7 purl divided by 1 double, 1 double, and repeat from * to the end of the lace.

40.—*Lace in Tatting and Crochet.*
Materials: Messrs. Walter Evans and Co.'s tatting cotton No. 50;
tatting-pin No. 2; crochet cotton No. 60.

40.—Lace in Tatting and Crochet.

The beauty of this lace depends entirely upon the regularity of the tatting. The purl stitches must be very regularly made, the circles must be drawn up tight. Make * 1 circle, consisting of 4 double, 8 purl divided by 2 double, 4 double; close to this circle a second one; 5 double fastened on the last purl of the preceding circle, 8 times 2 double divided by 1 purl, 1 purl 5 double, close to the 2nd circle a third one similar to the first, but instead of working the 1st purl fasten it on the last purl of the preceding circle; leave an interval of about 1-2/5 inch, and repeat from * till the lace is sufficiently long. The rest is worked in crochet. Take the fine crochet cotton and work the straight row at the top to join the patterns together. Crochet 1 double in the 3

first and last purl of the first and last circle of one pattern, then a
sufficient number of double stitches under the piece of cotton which
joins 2 circles. At the place where the circles are drawn together, join
the two pieces of cotton (the beginning and the end) in such a manner
that the top of the lace forms a straight line (see illustration). The 2nd
row consists of 1 treble in every other stitch, 1 chain after every treble.

Then work on the other side of the lace * a row of treble stitches
divided by chain. The treble stitches are worked in the purl stitches of
the circles. Work 1 long treble in the 1st purl left free of the 1st circle
(4th purl of the circle), 3 chain, * 1 treble, 3 chain, 1 treble, 3 chain, 2
treble in the next 2 purl, but cast off the 1st treble only so far as to
keep 2 loops on the needle. When the 2nd treble is completed cast off
all the loops on the needle, 3 chain, 5 treble divided by 4 chain, 3
chain, 2 treble in the 2 following purl, which are cast off like those
above described, 3 chain, 2 treble divided by 3 chain in the 2 next purl
of a pattern, 1 chain, 1 long treble with which you must join the last
purl and the first one of the next pattern, 1 chain; repeat from *. The
next row consists of small scallops worked round the chain stitch
scallops of the preceding row; work in each 1 double, 4 treble, 1
double, 1 double in the first and last chain stitch of every pattern.

41.—*Insertion in Tatting and Crochet.*
Materials: Messrs. Walter Evans and Co.'s tatting cotton No. 40;
crochet cotton No. 60; tatting-pin No. 2.

41.—Insertion in Tatting and Crochet.

Begin the tatting with fine cotton and 2 shuttles. Work with the cotton on one shuttle over the cotton on the other in the following manner:—Knot the 2 ends of cotton together * 4 times 2 double divided by a short purl, 3 long purl divided by 1 double; the 1st and 3rd purl must be three-fifths of an inch long, the 2nd one two-fifths of an inch; 4 times 2 double divided by a short purl, 1 purl two-fifths of an inch long; repeat from * till the strip of insertion is sufficiently long.

Then work a similar row of tatting, and join the two rows before working the 1 long purl, by fastening the cotton on the corresponding long purl of the 1st row, so that the 2 rows are joined closely together, and the purl stitches of either are turned outwards. At the top and bottom of the tatting work the 3 following rows of crochet:—* 1 double in the middle one of the 3 long purl, 8 chain, 1 double in each of the 3 following long purl, 8 chain; repeat from * to the end of the row. 2nd row. 8 double in each scallop, miss the 3 double stitches of the preceding row under 3 chain. The 3rd row consists of treble stitches in every other stitch, 1 chain after every treble. Lastly, the leaves are worked with thick cotton by filling up the first and last long purl of a pattern with darning stitch from illustration; the cross stitches between the two rows of tatting are worked with very fine cotton.

42.—*Purse in Tatting and Beads.*

Materials: Grey purse-silk; steel beads; scarlet glacé silk; a steel clasp with chain.

This purse is worked in tatting with grey silk and beads. The beads are threaded on a piece of silk, with which you work over another piece of the same. Begin each of the second halves of the purse with the circle in the centre, which consists of 1 purled stitch, 1 purl (all the purl of this circle are three-tenths of an inch long, and are covered with six beads, which must be drawn up close together before working the purl), 12 double divided by 1 purl. Join the stitches into a circle by knotting together the two ends of the silk.

2nd round: Begin again and work one of the small circles; * 2 double, draw up one bead after each, 1 double, 1 short purl without beads, 2 double, 1 bead after each, 1 double, fasten the silk on the purl of the middle circle, so as to let it come between the 3rd and 4th bead of the 6 beads on that purl; 2 double, 1 bead after each, 1 double, 1 short purl, 2 double, 1 bead after each, 1 double, join the stitches into a circle, draw up 2 beads; work a larger circle without fastening the silk belonging to the smaller one; 3 double, 1 bead after each, 1 double, 1 purl with 4 beads, 3 double, 1 bead after each, 1 double; 1 short purl, 3 double, 1 bead after each, 1 double, 1 purl with 4 beads, 3 double, 1 bead after each, 1 double; draw up 2 beads close to this large circle and repeat from *. Each following small circle must be fastened on the next purl of the circle which forms the centre; they are also fastened on to each other, instead of working the 1st purl, by fastening the piece of silk over which you work on the preceding small circle; in the larger circles, instead of working the 1st purl with 4 beads, the piece of silk must be fastened on the last purl of the preceding circle, so that it comes between the 2nd and 3rd beads. At the end of the round, the ends of the silk are knotted together and fastened off.

41.—Purse in Tatting and Beads.

3rd round: * 3 double, 1 bead after each, 1 double, 1 short purl, 3 double, 1 bead after each, 1 double fastened on the middle purl of the 1st circle of the preceding round, 3 double, 1 bead after each, 1 double, 1 purl with 2 beads, 3 double, 1 bead after each, 1 double; join the stitches into a circle, and work at a short distance a 2nd circle; 3 double, 1 bead after each, 1 double, fastened on the last purl of the just-finished circle of this round, 3 double, 1 bead after each, 1 double fastened on the purl of the preceding round which is between 2 circles; the loop must come between the 2 beads; 3 double, 1 bead after each; 1 double, 1 purl with 2 beads; 3 double, with 1 bead after each; 1 double; leave a small interval, and repeat 11 times more from *, then fasten the ends.

When two similar parts have been worked, line them with scarlet glacé silk; fasten them together round the outside, and sew on the clasp. A round of large circles edges the purse round the outside. The 1st of these circles consists of 12 double, 1 bead after each, 1 double, 1 purl with 2 beads, 4 double, 1 bead after each, 1 double. Work a 2nd circle at a short distance from the 1st: * 4 double, 1 bead after each, 1 double fastened on the purl of the 1st circle of this round; 7 double, 1 bead after each, 1 double, 1 purl with 2 beads, 4 double, 1 bead after each, 1 double; leave a short interval, and repeat from * till a sufficient number of circles have been made. The last purl is not worked in the last circle.

43.—*Insertion in Tatting and Crochet.*
>Materials: Messrs. Walter Evans and Co.'s tatting cotton No. 40; crochet cotton No. 60; tatting-pin No. 3.

43.—Insertion in Tatting and Crochet.

This pattern is composed of leaves and flowers. Each of the six leaves forming a circle is composed of 4 double, 2 purl, separated by 2 double, 4 double (the first and last purl of each leaf must be joined in the manner before explained), and the centre of each circle forms a wheel. The flower has four leaves: each leaf consists of 6 double, II purl, separated each by 1 double, and again 6 double; each leaf is filled up with button-hole stitches in fine cotton. To form the circle in the centre of this flower, turn several times the thread which joins the leaves, and work button-hole stitches round it. Join the flowers and the circles by knotting them together, or by making 1 purl longer than the others, and by drawing the next figure through. The crochet border on each side of the tatting consists of six rows, which are plainly seen in the illustration.

44.—*Border in Tatting and Lace Stitch.*
Materials: Messrs. Walter Evans and Co.'s tatting cotton No. 20 and
40.

44.—Border in Tatting and Lace Stitch.

This mixture of tatting and lace stitch is a style of work not only
entirely new, but very pretty and effective when cotton of very
different sizes is used. The tatting is begun with a row of circles
two-thirds of an inch distant from each other; each circle consists of
13 stitches of plain tatting. Fasten a 2nd row to the 1st, and a 3rd to
the 2nd, by working a circle of 13 stitches of plain tatting at one-third
of an inch distance, * then at the same distance; fasten the cotton on
the next circle of the preceding row, work a circle at the same distance
again, and repeat from *. The cotton is fastened on the circles by
drawing it through the circle with a crochet-needle, so as to form a
loop, and then drawing it out of the loop. Take care to keep the

distance between 2 circles always the same. Between the circles of the 3rd row draw another piece of cotton, by fastening the cotton on each circle of the 3rd row at distances of two-thirds of an inch. Then work the lower edge of the border in the following way:—1 small spot called a *Josephine knot* (for which work 5 stitches of plain tatting, draw the cotton downwards through the loop which fastens the stitches, and draw up the whole), fasten the cotton between the next two circles of the 3rd row, * and a little further make a spot consisting of 8 stitches of single tatting, close to this a circle formed of 3 double, 9 purl divided by 2 double, 3 double; then again a spot of 8 stitches of plain tatting, turn the 2 last spots so as to make their round sides come opposite one another; fasten the cotton on again between the 2 next circles of the 3rd row. Then a little further off work 1 small spot (5 stitches of plain tatting), 1 circle of 3 double, 1 purl, 2 double fastened on the last purl of the preceding circle, 2 double, 5 purl divided by 2 double, 3 double; then again a small spot (5 plain stitches), fasten the cotton on again between the next 2 circles of the 3rd row, and repeat from *, always fastening each new circle to the corresponding purl of the preceding one. On the other long side, the border is completed by 2 rows of crochet. The 1st row is formed by working 1 double under the piece of cotton between 2 circles of the 1st row, with 5 chain stitches between.

2nd row: 1 treble in every other stitch, 1 chain stitch after every treble. The strip of insertion is then tacked on a piece of cardboard or oil-cloth, and the lace stitches are worked between the circles, as is seen in illustration.

45.—*Tatted Rosette.*

Materials: Messrs. Walter Evans and Co.'s tatting cotton No. 30 for large rosette, No. 80 for small rosette; tatting-pin No. 3.

This rosette forms a very pretty trimming for lingerie—cravats, caps, handkerchiefs, &c. The raised pattern in the centre consists of 4 rounds, consisting of 5 circles each, which are sewn together and then fastened on the rosette. The 5 circles of each round must be worked close to each other: after working the last circle of each round, knot the beginning and end of the cotton together. Each circle of the smallest round has 9 double, the circles of the next round each 15, the circles of the following one 21, and the circles of the last and largest round 27 double stitches. When these circles have been sewn on one to another as in illustration, work a large circle consisting of 4 double, 1 purl, 9 times alternately 5 double, 1 purl, then 1 double. The purls of this circle are fastened on to the circles of the next round of the rosette. Fasten the cotton on to the next purl of the middle circle, and work a circle as follows:—4 double, 1 purl, 4 double, 1 purl, 3 double, 1 purl, 3 double, 1 purl, 4 double, 1 purl, 4 double. Repeat 9 times more from *, but now, instead of working the 1st purl of every circle, fasten it on to the last purl of the preceding circle. Then fasten the cotton. For the last round, which consists of scallops and rounds, fasten the cotton on to the middle purl of a circle of the preceding round, and work a circle consisting of 3 times alternately 4 double, 1 purl, then 4 double.

45.—Tatted Rosette.

Then fasten a second thread on to the same purl on which the just completed circle has been fastened, and over which all the scallops are to be worked. Work over it 5 double, fastened on to the last purl of the preceding circle, 4 double, 1 purl, 4 double, 1 purl, 5 double. Fasten the cotton on to the middle purl of the next circle of the preceding round, and repeat from * till the round is completed; but in working these circles, instead of the first purl, fasten them on to the last purl of the preceding scallop. Lastly, the raised pattern is sewn on.

46.—*Linen Bag for Tatting, &c.*

Materials: Fine linen; Messrs. Walter Evans and Co.'s tatting cotton No. 30 or 40; tatting-pin No. 2.

46.—Linen Bag for Tatting, &c.

This pretty linen bag is meant to keep tatting and such work from being soiled before it is completed. The bag is drawn together round the top. Its size depends upon what you wish to put into it. The original pattern is 3-3/4 inches deep, and 3 inches wide; it is hemmed round the top, and trimmed with a narrow tatted lace, consisting of large and small circles.

47.—Tatted Border.
Materials: Messrs. Walter Evans and Co.'s tatting cotton No. 40; tatting-pin No. 2.

47.—Tatted Border.

Begin this elegant border with 2 rows of tatting, in the following manner:—

1st row: 2 double, 1 purl, 3 double, 1 purl, 3 double, 1 purl, 2 double; draw these stitches up into a circle, and repeat the circle at a very short distance, till the border is long enough; but instead of working the first purl of each circle, you must join the circle to the preceding one; the purl on the sides of the circle must therefore be longer than that in the middle.

For the 2nd row take another shuttle, make a loop on the left side with the cotton, and work with this end of cotton over the cotton in the right hand, which is also to be held between the thumb and forefinger of the left hand. Then work in the following way:—2 double, then 1 circle consisting of 3 double, 1 purl, 3 double; to form this circle, let the cotton in the left-hand shuttle fall downwards, and make a loop round the left hand with the cotton on the shuttle of the right hand. Then take up again the left-hand shuttle, and join the circle to the middle purl of the 1st circle of the 1st row by drawing the cotton through the purl like a loop, and then drawing the cotton in the right hand through this loop. * 7 double, 1 circle, 7 double, joined to the middle purl of the next circle of the 1st row; 1 circle, 5 double, 1 circle joined on the middle purl of the following circle; repeat from *.

The upper edge of the border is worked in 2 crochet rows, in the following manner:—

1st row: * 2 treble, divided by 1 chain in the 1st circle of the 1st row of tatting; 2 chain; repeat from *.

2nd row: * 1 treble in the 1st chain of the preceding row, 1 purl (3 chain, 1 slip stitch in the 1st), miss 1 stitch of the preceding row under it; repeat from *.

48.—*Rosette in Embroidery and Tatting.*
Materials for trimmings: Messrs. Walter Evans and Co.'s knitting cotton No. 20; tatting cotton No. 50; tatting-pin No. 3. For couvrettes, crochet cotton No. 4.

This rosette, joined to other similar ones, forms a very pretty trimming for articles of fine linen, or even for small couvrettes; if used for the former, they must be worked with very fine cotton. The centre of the rosette is formed of an embroidered raised pattern worked in *point de minute*; round this centre there are small circles worked in button-hole stitch; the embroidery is worked with knitting cotton, the circles with crochet cotton. Before beginning the circles, make a circle consisting of a foundation chain of 80 stitches, in order to be able to fasten the button-hole stitch; in each of the stitches of the foundation chain work 1 double, then fasten the cotton. In the 2nd round of these circles fasten the cotton on every 5th stitch of the crochet circle. Work 1 round of open-work treble stitch in the double stitch of the crochet circle, work in tatting the border of the rosette as follows in 1 round:—* 2 double, 1 purl, 2 double, fastened on to 1 chain stitch between 2 treble stitch, 2 double; 1 purl, 2 double,; join these stitches into a circle; turn the work so that the wrong side lies upwards, and work a second larger circle at a short distance consisting of 4 double, 5 purl divided by 2 double, 4 double, turn again and repeat from *. The smaller circles must be fastened after every other treble stitch; the larger and smaller circles must be fastened above one another at the place of the 1st purl.

48.—Rosette in Embroidery and Tatting.

49—Linen Collar trimmed with Tatting.
Materials: Messrs. Walter Evans and Co's tatting cotton No. 60; tatting-pin No. 2.

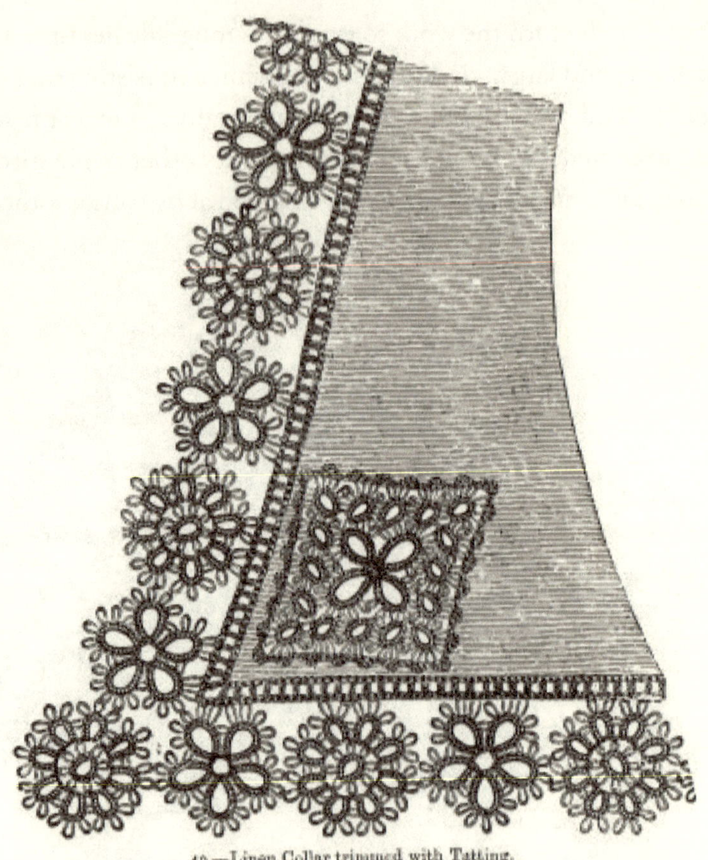

49.—Linen Collar trimmed with Tatting.

The diamond pattern placed in the corner of the collar is commenced in the centre. For each of the four centre leaves work 6 double stitches, 6 purl divided one from the other by 3 double stitches, then 6 more double stitches. Fasten off the cotton, cut it, and begin a fresh leaf by working 2 double stitches, 10 purl divided one from the other by 2 double stitches, then 2 more double stitches. (This small leaf forms one of the corners of the diamond pattern.) Fasten the cotton to the fourth purl of one of the four centre leaves, and work another leaf similar to the preceding. Join this leaf by its two centre purl to the two last purl of the corner leaf (see illustration). After two more similar leaves, work one corner leaf, and continue the pattern in the same manner until you come back to the first corner leaf, then fasten off, and cut the cotton. Place the diamond pattern upon the point of the collar, and cut away the material under it; fold back the edges, sew them neatly, and cover them with the following crochet edging:—Make alternately 2 chain, 1 purl (the latter composed of 3 chain joined together by 1 slip stitch). It will be easy to work the circles in tatting from our illustration; they form an elegant border round the collar. We shall merely say that the centre circle is always worked separately, and that the cotton is fastened on afresh to work the eight outer leaves. The upper edge of this border is worked in crochet. It is composed of two rows—one formed of chain stitches, and a few slip stitches worked in the purl of the circles in tatting, the other worked in open treble crochet.

50.—*Cravat in Cambric Muslin and Tatting.*
Materials: Messrs. Walter Evans and Co.'s tatting cotton No. 100; tatting-pin No. 3.
This cravat consists of a strip of cambric muslin 1 yard long, 6 inches wide, hemmed on both sides. The ends of the cravat are ornamented with patterns in tatting, worked with tatting cotton No. 100. A rosette in tatting is sewn on in the middle of the end of the cravat. The end of the cravat is pointed, lined on the wrong side with a strip of the same material as the cravat, and edged with a tatted lace.

50.—Cravat in Muslin and Tatting.

Begin the rosette in the centre with a circle worked in the following manner:—1 double, 1 purl, * twice 2 double divided by 1 purl, 1 purl, 3 double, 1 purl, twice 4 double divided by 1 purl, 1 purl, * 3 double, 1 purl; repeat from * to * once more, 2 double. At the beginning of the 2nd round fasten the cotton on the 1st purl of the 1st round, and work as follows:—* 1 circle consisting of 10 double, 1 purl, 2 double, 1 purl, 10 double; fasten the cotton on to the next purl, 1 circle like the preceding one, fastened on to the next purl, 1 circle consisting of 9 double, 1 purl, 9 double fastened on to the next purl, 2 circles consisting each of 7 double, 1 purl, 7 double; between the 2 fasten the cotton on to the next purl; 2 similar circles fastened also on to the next purl, 1 circle consisting of 8 double, 1 purl, 8 double, fastened on to the next circle; repeat once more from *, and fasten off the cotton. Fasten on the cotton afresh for the 3rd round, worked in the following manner:—* 1 circle consisting of 6 double, 1 purl, 5 double, 1 purl, 6 times 2 double divided by 1 purl; 1 purl, 5 double, 1 purl, 6 double; fasten the cotton at a short distance on to the 1st purl of the 2nd round, 1 circle worked as follows:—5 double fastened on to the last purl of the preceding circle of this round, 4 double, 1 purl, 4 times 2 double divided by 1 purl, 1 purl, 4 double, 1 purl, 5 double fastened on to the next purl of the 2nd circle of the 2nd round; 6 similar circles, between each of which the cotton is to be fastened on to the nearest purl of a circle of the 2nd round; repeat once more from *, and knot the beginning and the end of the cotton together. When completed, the rosette is sewn on the material of the cravat with button-hole stitches, taking up one purl with each stitch; the muslin is cut away underneath the rosette; then work a round of knotted stitches underneath the button-hole stitch. For the lace, make a row of circles one-fifth of an inch distant from each other, consisting each of 6 double, 1 purl, 2 double, 1 purl, 4 times 2 double divided by 1 purl, 1 purl, 2 double, 1 purl, 6 double, which are fastened together by the purl of each circle, and are sewn on the cravat over the cotton between the circles in overcast stitch.

51—*Cravat in Cambric Muslin and Tatting.*
Materials: Messrs. Walter Evans and Co.'s tatting cotton No. 100; tatting-pin No. 3.

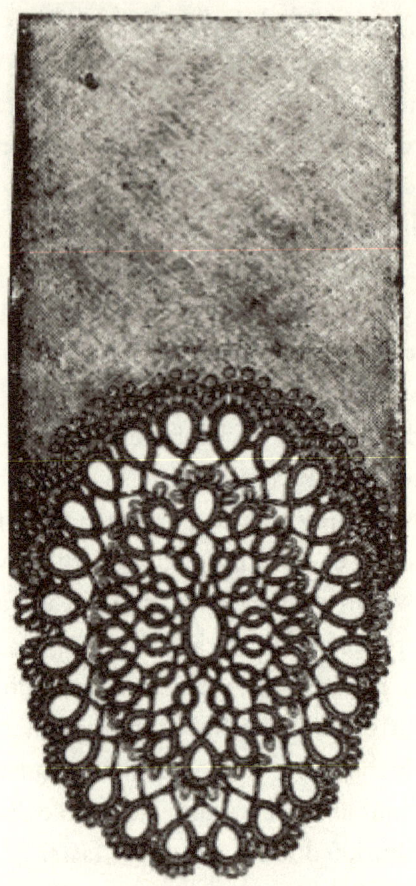

51,—Cravat in Muslin and Tatting.

The end of this cravat is formed by a long rosette or *médaillon* in tatting. This rosette is likewise begun in the centre, and consists of 4 rounds, the 2 first of which are worked like those of the rosette in illustration 50, with this difference only, that in the 2nd round each of the circles nearest to the top and to the bottom of the rosette consists of 8 double, 1 purl, 2 double, 1 purl, 8 double. 3rd round: * 1 circle, consisting of 6 double, 1 purl, 5 double, 1 purl, 6 times 2 double divided by 1 purl, 1 purl, 5 double, 1 purl, 6 double, fastened on to the next purl of the 2nd circle of the preceding round; 1 circle as follows:—5 double, the last of which is fastened on to the last purl of the preceding round, 4 double, 1 purl, twice 2 double divided by 1 purl, 1 purl, 4 double, 1 purl, 5 double fastened on the next purl of the preceding round; 8 more similar circles, between each of which the cotton is fastened on to the next purl of the preceding round; repeat from * once more, fasten the two ends of the cotton together. 4th round: * Fasten on the cotton afresh with a circle consisting of 7 double, 1 purl, 4 double, 1 purl, 6 times 2 double divided by 1 purl, 1 purl, 4 double, 1 purl, 7 double, fastened on to the middle purl of the 1st circle of the preceding round; a 2nd circle worked in the same way, only instead of working the last purl, fasten the cotton on to the last purl of the preceding circle, then on to the 1st circle of the preceding round; 10 more similar circles, between each of which the cotton is fastened on to the middle purl of a circle of the preceding round, and then on to the 2nd purl of the larger circle at the bottom of the medallion; repeat once more from *. The pattern is sewn on the cravat with button-hole stitches, as can be seen in the illustration.

52.—Border in Crochet and Tatting.
Materials: Messrs. Walter Evans and Co.'s Boar's Head cotton No. 26.

52.—Border in Crochet and Tatting.

This border is formed of circles in tatting and crochet leaves, which are joined together by rows of crochet work; a narrow border in tatting forms the lower edge. Omitting this edge, the border forms a strip of insertion. Each of the rosettes or circles is begun in the centre; work first 2 double (a double stitch is formed by passing the thread over the back of the hand, and then passing the shuttle upwards between the forefinger and second finger, and drawing it up, then work a stitch of plain tatting; this completes the double stitch, and whenever so many double stitches are directed it means the 2 stitches), 1 purl, repeat 9 times, join the stitch into a circle, work at a small distance * a smaller ring consisting of 3 double, 5 purl, divided each by 2 double stitches, 4 double, draw the cotton through the purl of the first circle, and repeat 8 times more from *, only each following circle must be fastened on to a purl of the preceding circle after 3 double stitches, and having completed each circle the thread must be drawn through the purl of the first circle, which forms the centre of the rosette. The beginning and the end of the thread are knotted together. For the tatted border, make at short distances 1 loop with 5 double, 1 purl, 5 double; after having worked a sufficient number of such loops, wind another thread round the thread between the loops, turning always 1 loop on the right side and 1 on the left. Now begin the crochet part with the leaves. Make for each of these a foundation chain of 12 stitches, crochet back over this chain 2 double in the last stitch but one, 1 double in the next stitch, 1 treble in each of the following 7 chain, 2 treble in the next stitch, 2 treble, 1 long treble, and 2 treble in the next following stitch of the foundation chain. Work on the other side of the chain the same pattern, only the reverse way; then 3 double in the point of the leaf thus formed, and edge the whole leaf with a round of double stitches, always working 2 double in each stitch of the preceding row, and 3 in the long treble stitch. In working this last round, the circles must be joined to the leaves by taking up the purl stitch of the circle before casting off the corresponding double stitch of the leaf; then work the stem which joins the 2 rows of circles and leaves with a row of chain stitches, on which a row of double is worked. Then comes the border which forms the upper edge. Make a row of chain stitches, joining leaves and circles together, then work 3 rows of treble, work 3 more rows over the tatted border, the first row entirely in chain stitches, after every fourth stitch take up the purl of the loops on one side. 2nd row: 1 treble in the middle stitch of the 3 chain, 2 treble, divided by 3 chain. 3rd row: 1 treble, 1 chain, miss 1 under the last. In the last row the leaves and circles must be fastened on the border, as seen in illustration.

53.—*Diamond in Tatting.*

Materials: Messrs. Walter Evans and Co.'s crochet cotton No. 10; tatting-pin No. 2; any sized shuttle.

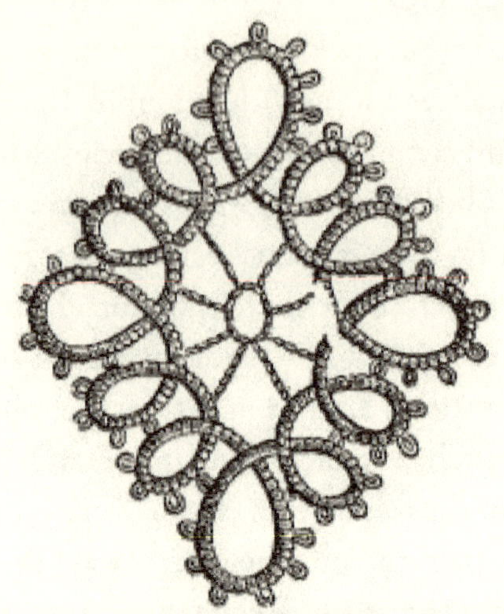

53.—Diamond in Tatting.

1st oval: Fill the shuttle, but do not cut it off from the reel, as a double thread is required, and commence by working 5 double stitches, 1 purl, then (3 double, 1 purl 10 times), 5 double, draw up.

Double thread: Putting the thread attached to the reel round the left hand, work 7 single stitches, taking care to do them tightly.

2nd oval: 4 double, join to the last purl of 1st oval, then (3 double, 1 purl, 5 times) 4 double, draw up.

Double thread: 12 single stitches tightly worked.

3rd oval: 4 double, join to last purl of 2nd oval, 3 double, join to next purl of 2nd oval, then (3 double, 1 purl 5 times) 4 double, draw up.

Double thread: 12 single stitches.

4th oval: 4 double, join to last purl of last oval, 3 double, join to next purl, then (3 double, 1 purl, 8 times) 4 double, draw up.

Double thread: 12 single stitches.

5th oval: 4 double, join to last purl of last oval, 3 double, join to next purl, then (3 double, 1 purl, 5 times) 4 double, draw up.

Double thread: 12 single stitches.

6th oval: 4 double, join to last purl of last oval, 3 double, join to next purl, then (3 double, 1 purl, 4 times) 4 double, draw up.

Double thread: 7 single stitches.

7th oval: 5 double, join to last purl of last oval, then (3 double, 1 purl, 10 times) 5 double, draw up.

Double thread: 7 single stitches.

8th oval: 4 double, join to last purl of last oval, then (3 double, 1 purl, 5 times) 4 double, draw up.

Double thread: 12 single stitches.

9th oval: 4 double, join to last purl of last oval, 3 double, join to next purl then (3 double, 1 purl, 5 times) 4 double, draw up.

Double thread: 12 single stitches.

10th oval: 4 double, join to last purl of last oval, 3 double, join to next purl, then (3 double, 1 purl, 8 times) 4 double, draw up.

Double thread: 12 single stitches.

11th oval: 4 double, join to last purl of last oval, 3 double, join to next purl, then (3 double, 1 purl, 5 times) 4 double, draw up.

Double thread: 12 single stitches.

12th oval: 4 double, join to last purl of last oval, 3 double, join to next purl, then (3 double, 1 purl, 3 times) 3 double, join to 1st purl of 1st oval, 4 double, draw up.

Double thread: 7 single stitches.

Now cut off both threads, and with a needle fasten off neatly at the back of first oval by sewing 1 thread over the other.

The diamond is now finished. The centre must be filled up with lacework, using fine sewing-cotton.

Arranged in groups of 7 or 8, 3 diamonds form a very pretty trimming for the skirts of silk dresses, the body being trimmed with single diamonds.

54.—Linen Collar trimmed with Tatting.

Materials: Messrs. Walter Evans and Co.'s tatting cotton No. 100,
tatting-pin No. 3; 1 piece of very fine cord.

This collar is ornamented with a triangle and a border of a very
effective pattern. The triangle is begun in the centre, by working for
each of the three leaves 5 double stitches, 5 purl divided one from the
other by 2 double stitches, and 5 more double stitches. When the
third leaf is completed, fasten off and cut the cotton. Now take,
instead of the cotton wound upon the shuttle, a piece of extremely fine
cord, over which work with the cotton from the reel the following row
of stitches:—1 double stitch, fasten the cotton to the centre purl of
one of the three leaves, * 2 double stitches, 5 purl divided one from the
other by 2 double stitches, 3 double stitches, fasten the cotton to the
centre purl of the nearest leaf, 2 double stitches, 9 purl divided one
from the other by 3 double stitches, 2 double stitches fastened to the
same purl as before. Repeat from * twice more, then fasten off, and cut
the cord and the cotton. Begin afresh, and work 3 small circles, each
composed of 12 plain stitches placed quite close together (these form
one of the corners of the triangle), then at small distances one from
the other work 13 similar circles, every second one of which is
fastened to one purl of the row of stitches worked over the cord (see
illustration). Cut away from the collar the piece of linen which is to be
replaced by the triangle, fold in the edges and work them round in
button-hole stitch, and fill up the space with the triangle. For the
border, work first * one circle composed of 3 double stitches, 4 purl
divided one from the other by 2 double stitches, 3 more double
stitches; take up the cord once more and work over it, 3 double
stitches, then, without cord, 1 circle composed of 2 double stitches, 12
purl divided one from the other by 2 double stitches, 2 more double
stitches; take up the cord again and work over it 3 double stitches, 4
purl divided each by 2 double stitches, 3 double stitches. Fasten the
cotton to the third purl (reckoning from the last) of the second circle
worked without cord; 3 double stitches fastened to the fourth purl of

the row of stitches worked over the cord (see illustration), 2 double stitches, 6 purl divided each by 2 double stitches, 3 double stitches fastened to the purl of next circle, 3 double stitches fastened to the last purl of the row, 2 double stitches, 3 purl divided each by 2 double stitches, 3 double stitches; fasten the cotton to the sixth purl of the circle (reckoning from the beginning), 4 double stitches. Repeat from *. Work over the top of the border a crochet edging similar to that round the diamond pattern of collar No. 49. For the point of the border, at the corner of the collar, see illustration No. 54.

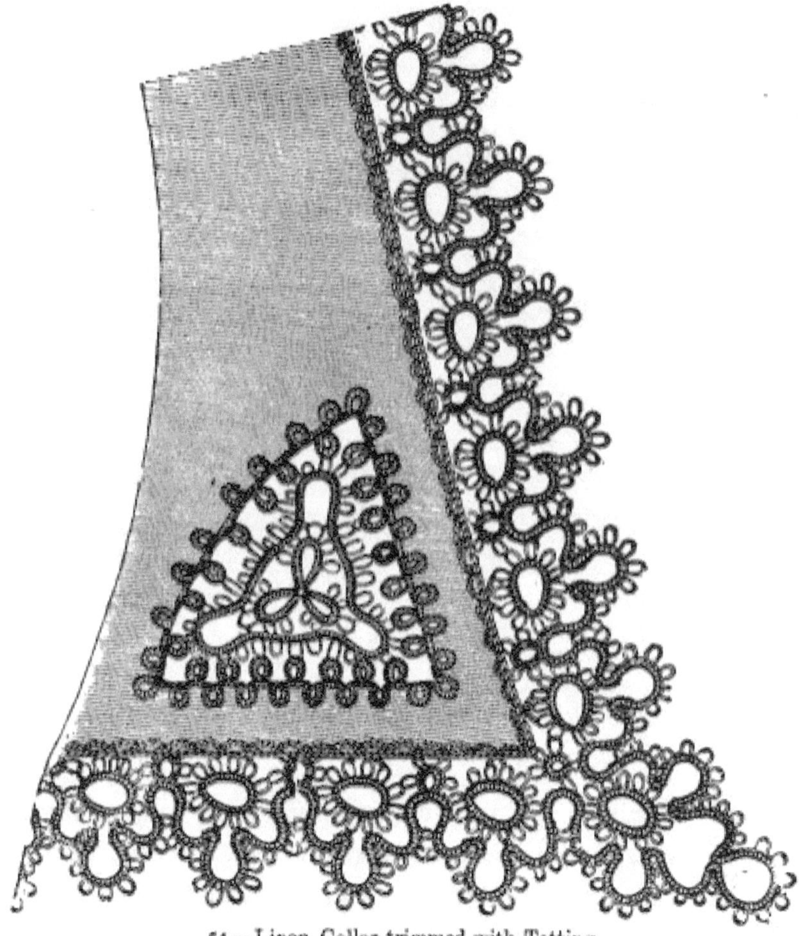

54.—Linen Collar trimmed with Tatting.

55.—Tatted Collar.

Materials: Messrs. Walter Evans and Co.'s tatting cotton No. 100;
tatting-pin No. 1.

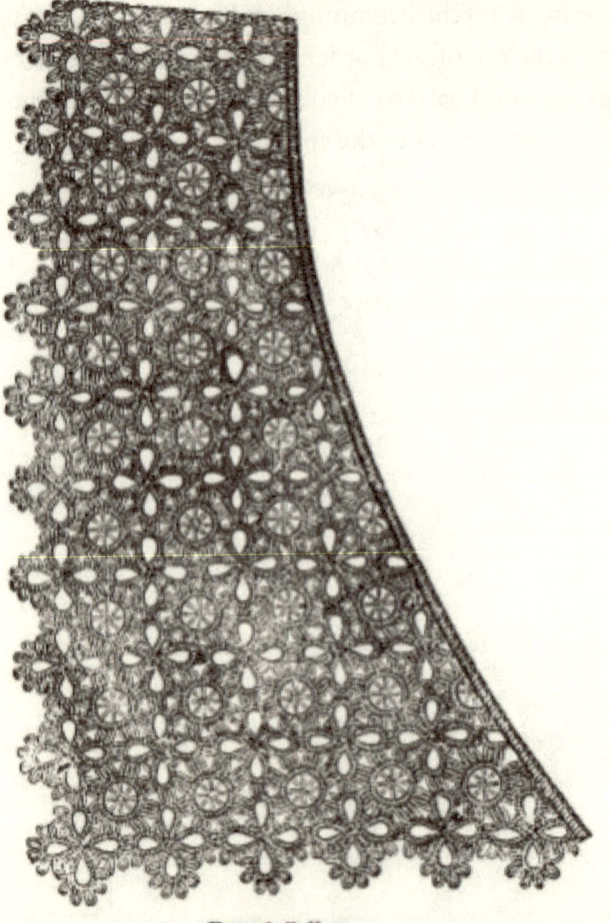

55.—Tatted Collar.

This collar is worked with very fine tatting cotton. It consists of four
branched tatted patterns and of separate tatted circles, fastened on to
one another as seen in illustration. The four branched patterns are
worked as follow:—3 double, 1 purl, 7 times alternately 2 double, 1

purl, then 3 double, and join the knots into a circle. Work 3 similar leaves close to this 1st leaf, but instead of working the 1st purl, fasten them on to the last purl of the preceding leaf; besides this, instead of working the last purl of the 4th branch, fasten it on to the first purl of the 1st branch. When 1 such four-branched pattern is completed, knot both ends of the cotton together and cut them off. Make a row of similar patterns by joining them on to the 2 middle purl of a branch of the preceding pattern, instead of working the 2 middle purl of the last branch (see illustration). Two rows of similar patterns are joined by the above-mentioned circles, consisting of 32 double stitches, by fastening these circles from illustration between four branched patterns. Begin each circle with 2 double stitches, fasten it on to the corresponding purl of the four-branched pattern, work again 2 double, fasten on to the next purl, and continue in the same manner till the circle is sufficiently large. Each circle is ornamented with lace stitch. The collar is edged round the neck with close button-hole stitches.

56.—*Tatted Collar.*

Materials: Messrs. Walter Evans and Co.'s tatting cotton No. 60; tatting-pin No. 3.

This collar is commenced at the top, and worked with fine cotton in the following manner:—1st oval: 2 double, 1 purl, 9 times, draw the cotton into a circle, 3 double, 1 purl, 1 double, 5 times, 1 purl, 3 double, draw the cotton into a circle, and join it to the first purl of the first circle; work two more circles the same as last. 2nd oval: 2 double, 1 purl, 7 times, join the third purl to the third purl of the centre circle of preceding pattern, 3 double, 1 purl, 3 times, 2 double, 1 purl, draw the cotton up, and work 5 small circles, as follow:—3 double *, 1 purl, 1 double, 4 times, * 1 purl, 3 double, joining each circle to the purl of the 2nd oval. 3rd oval: 2 double, 1 purl, 8 times, joining the 3rd purl to the 2nd purl of the centre circle of the preceding pattern, 3 double,

1 purl, 4 times, 2 double, 1 purl, draw the cotton up, and work 7 small circles, similar to the small circles described in 2nd oval.

56.—Tatted Collar.

57.—*Circle in Tatting.*
Materials: Messrs. Walter Evans and Co's tatting cotton No. 50; tatting-pin No. 2.

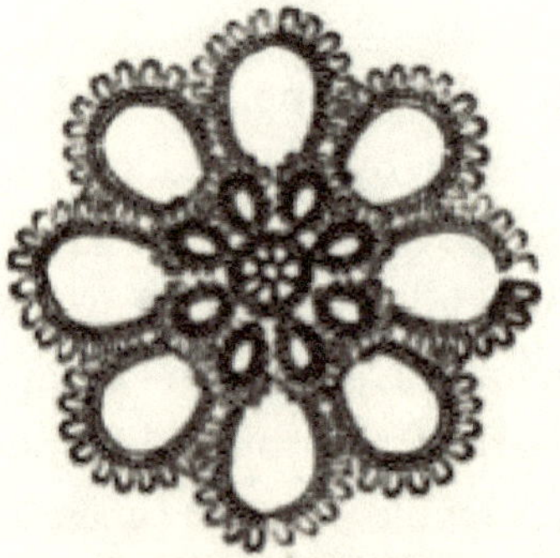

57.—Circle in Tatting.

This circle is worked with fine cotton, and will be very pretty for ornamenting cravat-ends and different articles of lingerie. It is commenced in the centre with 2 double, 1 purl, repeated 8 times, draw the cotton into a ring, and work 8 small circles, as follow:—3 double, * 1 purl, 1 double, repeat from * 6 times, 1 purl, 3 double, draw up the cotton, and join it to the purl of centre ring and corresponding circle. Large circle: 3 double, * 1 purl, 2 double, repeat from * 14 times, 3 double, draw up the cotton, and join it to the 4th purl of small circle. The centre of ring is filled up with lace stitches.

58.—*Tatting Medallion for Trimming Lingeries, &c.c.*
Materials: Messrs. Walter Evans and Co.'s tatting cotton No. 50 for cravats and collars, 100 for pocket-handkerchiefs, 20 for petticoats; tatting-pin No. 2 or 3.

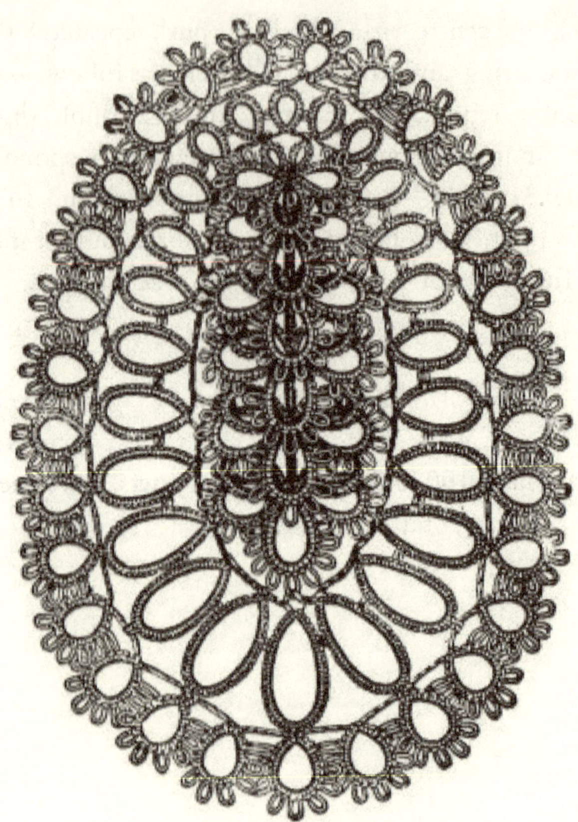

58.—Tatting Medallion.

This pattern is suitable for trimming cravats, collars, pocket-handkerchiefs, petticoats, &c.c., according to the size of the cotton with which it is worked. Work first the round of circles which incloses the leaves, overlapping each other in the centre; begin with the smallest circle, which is at the top of the pattern; it consists of 3 double, 1 purl, 7 double, 1 purl, 7 double, 1 purl, 3 double. Then work at a short distance another circle like the preceding one, only work 8 double instead of 7, and instead of working the first purl, fasten the circle on to the last purl of the preceding circle; all the other circles are fastened on to each other in the same manner. The next circle, worked again at a distance of about one-fifth of an inch, has 4 double; fasten it on to the preceding circle, 9 double, 1 purl, 9 double, 1 purl, 4 double. The following four circles are worked like the preceding one; only work in the first of these circles 10 double instead of 9, in the second 11 double, in the third 12 double. The piece of cotton which joins the circles together must also be somewhat longer between the larger circles. Then work a circle as follows: 5 double, fasten the cotton, 13 double, 1 purl, 13 double, 1 purl, 5 double; then a similar circle, but always working 14 double instead of 13. The next circle consists of 6 double, fasten the cotton, 15 double, 1 purl, 15 double, 1 purl, 6 double; the two following circles are worked in the same manner, working 16 double instead of 15. Then comes the largest circle of the round, which consists of 6 double, 17 double, 1 purl, 17 double, 1 purl, 6 double. Work 11 circles more like the 2nd to 12th of those just described (the 13th circle forms the middle), only the order of sizes must be reversed, so that the round closes with the smallest circle. Then fasten both ends of the cotton together, so that the circles are joined into a circle. Then work round this row of circles another round, the circles of which must be of graduated sizes like those of the first round. Fasten the cotton on to the middle purl of the first small circle of the first round, and work one circle as follows:—3 double, 1 purl, 6 times alternately 2 double, 1 purl, then 3 double; fasten the cotton on to the middle purl of the next circle, &c.c. The remaining circles are worked in the same manner, only they must be increased and decreased in size gradually like the circles of the first round; this is done by increasing or decreasing the number of purl, instead of working the first purl of every following circle, fasten it on to the last purl of the preceding circle. When the round is completed, fasten both ends of the cotton together. In the centre of the oval pattern, fasten 6 five-branched patterns of graduated size, which are worked in one piece. For the smallest of these patterns work first three circles, consisting of 5 double, 1 purl, 5 times alternately 2 double, 1 purl, then again 5 double (these circles must be close to each other; the second and third circles must, moreover, be fastened on to the last purl of the preceding circle). The cotton is then fastened on the first circle between the beginning and the end of the same, then work close to them two small circles, consisting of 6 double, 1 purl, 6 double, fasten the cotton between the beginning and the end of the third circle. The other five-branched patterns are worked in the same manner at intervals of about three-tenths of an inch; but the separate circles of each pattern must become gradually larger. In the largest pattern the three large circles consist of 5 double, 1 purl, 8 times alternately 2 double, 1 purl, 5 double; the two smaller circles consist each of 15 double, 1 purl, 15 double; the size of the other patterns can easily be worked from this; the cotton which joins these last together is covered by over-casting with a needle and thread, so as to imitate double stitches. The five-branched patterns are then fastened in the oval pattern; they must overlap each other to half way, as seen in the illustration.

59.—*Tatted Diamond.*

Materials: Messrs. Walter Evans and Co.'s tatting cotton No. 40, or 80 if required finer; tatting-pin No. 3.

59.—Tatted Diamond.

This pattern is meant to ornament lingerie; it is worked with fine tatting cotton in the following manner:—Work a * circle consisting of 6 double, 1 purl, 6 double, turn the circle downwards and work at a short distance another circle consisting of 5 double, 4 purl divided by 2 double, 5 double; at a similar distance a circle of 5 double fastened on to the last purl of the preceding circle, 2 double, 5 purl divided by 2 double, 5 double; then again a circle consisting of 5 double fastened on to the last purl of the preceding circle, 2 double, 3 purl divided by 2 double, 5 double: fasten the cotton on to the first circle. Then turn the work so that the last three circles are turned downwards, leave an interval of at least three-fourths of an inch, and repeat three times more from *, fastening the circles on to each other from illustration. Knot together the beginning and end of the cotton, work button-hole stitches round the cotton which joins the circles, as shown in illustration. The purl stitches of the four middle circles of the diamond are knotted together.

60.—*Tatted Cravat End.*

Materials: Messrs. Walter Evans and Co.'s tatting cotton No. 50; tatting-pin No. 3; 2 shuttles.

This cravat end is given in full size. It is ornamented with a tatted medallion, edged with lace. The tatting is worked with tatting fine cotton and two shuttles. Make first the two rosettes which form the centre of the medallion, then the insertion-like part which edges the rosettes. The larger rosette is worked as follows:—Knot the cotton of both shuttles together and work with 1 shuttle only 1 circle consisting of 10 double, 1 purl one-fifth of an inch long, 10 double; * close to this circle, which is turned downwards, work over the cotton with the other shuttle, 1 double, 1 purl, 8 double; this forms one of the scallops joining two circles. Then turn the work again and work close to the just completed scallop another circle like the first, but which is joined to the first circle instead of working the purl. Repeat 4 times more from *. Then work another scallop and fasten both ends of cotton on to the cotton over which the first scallop has been worked, at the place where the scallop is joined to the first circle. The first round of the rosette is thus completed.

Work then the 2nd round over the cotton on the 2nd shuttle, beginning to work where the two ends of cotton have been fastened, * 6 double, 1 purl, 5 double, fastened on to the purl of the next scallop of the preceding round, 5 double, 1 purl, 6 double fastened on to the cotton between two scallops of the preceding round; repeat 5 times more from *. The larger rosette is now completed. The smaller rosette is worked like the first, only without the second round. The insertion-like border is worked in two halves as follows:—The half which touches the edge of the medallion is worked as follows:—Knot both ends of cotton together and *, work with 1 shuttle only 1 circle consisting of 8 double, 1 purl one-fifth of an inch long, 8 double; turn the circle downwards and work close to it over the cotton on the 2nd shuttle 6 double, 1 purl, 6 double; this forms a scallop of the border.

Then turn the work again and work close to the scallop another circle like the first, but which is fastened on to the first circle instead of working the purl. Turn the work again, work a scallop like the preceding one, and repeat 15 times more from *, only the scallops at the lower edge of the medallion must have a few double stitches more, as can be seen in illustration. After working the last scallop fasten the two ends of the cotton on to the 1st circle; then cut them off. The second inner half is worked like the first; only the circles are worked without any purl stitch, and fastened on to the circles of the first half from illustration; the scallops of this half are somewhat smaller; each consists of 5 double, 1 purl, 5 double. The completed border is sewn on to the rosettes from illustration; the different pieces must be first fastened on cardboard. The cotton must be wound several times round the long threads, as seen in illustration. The medallion is then sewn into the muslin at the top only; the remaining border is edged, before joining it to the muslin, with a straight row of knots to be worked over cotton, and fastened on to each outer scallop of the border at regular intervals. The number of double stitches between two purl is different, as distinctly seen in illustration. For the lace knot both ends of cotton together, * work with one shuttle only 1 circle consisting of 8 double, 1 purl, 8 double; turn the work and make another circle consisting of 2 double, 9 times alternately 1 purl, 2 double; then fasten this circle on to the preceding one, where it has been joined into a circle, so that both circles meet as seen in illustration. After having turned the work again, work 9 double over the cotton on the 2nd shuttle, which form a scallop between the circles, and repeat from *. The lace is then sewn round the edge of the muslin.

61.—Rosette in Tatting and Embroidery.
Materials: Messrs. Walter Evans and Co.'s tatting cotton No. 60, or No. 40 if desired in a larger size.

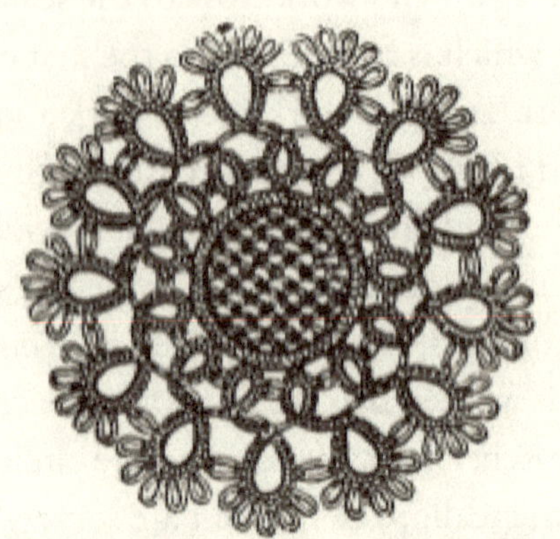

61.—Rosette in Tatting and Embroidery.

This rosette is suitable for ornamenting lingeries, cravats, &c.c. It is worked in white embroidery and lace stitch, and edged all round with a tatted lace. For the latter work with very fine cotton * 1 large circle, consisting of 5 double, 1 purl, 7 times alternately 2 double, 1 purl, then 5 double. At a short distance from this circle work a smaller one, consisting of 5 double fastened on to the last purl of the large circle, 5 double. Leave again an interval as small as the last, and repeat from * 11 times more. But in working the large circles, instead of working the 1st purl, fasten them on the same purl of the large circle on which the small circle has been fastened; besides this, in working the last (12th) large circle, instead of working the last purl, fasten it on the 1st purl of the 1st circle; the last small circle is fastened on to the same purl. The lace is thus joined into a circle, and is sewn round the outside of the rosette with button-hole stitches.

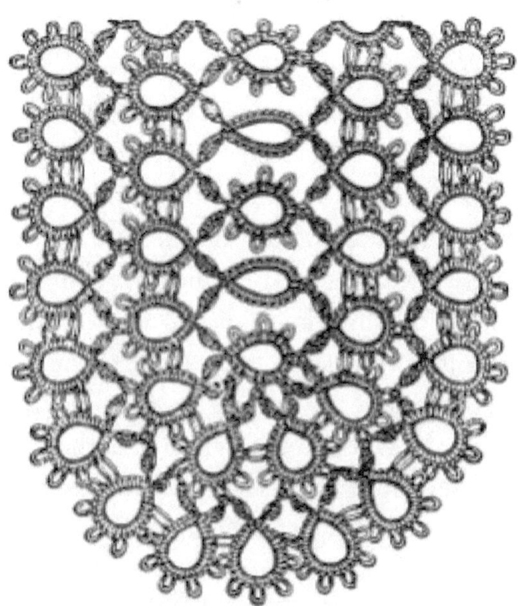

62.—Cravat End in Tatting.

62—Cravat End in Tatting.
Materials: Messrs. Walter Evans and Co.'s tatting cotton No. 60;
tatting-pin No. 3.
The illustration shows the end of a tatted cravat. Work first the middle
row of the cravat at the same time with the row of circles on the left
side of the middle row in illustration; begin with the first circle of the
middle row. It consists of 7 times alternately 3 double, 1 small purl,
then 3 double. Work close to this circle, which must be turned
downwards, a Josephine knot, consisting of 5 plain stitches, then a
circle consisting of 5 double, 1 purl one-fifth of an inch long, 5 times
alternately 3 double, 1 small purl; 3 double, 1 long purl, 5 double.
*Turn this circle (which is the first of the side row) downwards, work
close to it a Josephine knot, then a circle consisting of 12 double, 1
small purl, 12 double. Turn this circle downwards, work a Josephine
knot, and then again a circle like the first of the side row, but instead

of working the first long purl, fasten it on to the last purl of the preceding circle of the same row. Then hold the work so that the circles of the side row are turned downwards, work a Josephine knot, 1 circle like the first circle of the middle row, turn the work, make 1 Josephine knot, and then a circle like the second circle of the side row. Repeat from * till the cravat is sufficiently long. The last circle of the middle row must correspond to the first circle of the same row. Then begin to work the lower edge at the same time with the last circle of the middle row, * 1 Josephine knot, then a circle like the circles of the side row, again 1 Josephine knot, fastened on to the next purl of the last circle of the middle row; repeat 3 times more from *. Then continue as before, and work on the right side of the middle row a row of circles exactly like those which have been worked at the same time with those of the middle row.

The fastening on of the cotton between two Josephine knots is seen in illustration. The circles at the other end of the cravat are fastened like those of the first-described end. The cravat is edged all round with a row of circles with Josephine knots worked exactly like those of the preceding row, and the manner of fastening which is seen in the illustration.

63.—*Rosette in Tatting and Embroidery.*
Materials: Messrs. Walter Evans and Co.'s tatting cotton No. 60, or 40 if required larger; tatting-pin No. 3.

63.—Rosette in Tatting and Embroidery.

The centre of this rosette is worked in lace stitch on muslin, edged round with button-hole stitch and trimmed with a tatted lace, which is worked at the same time with the centre. Work first * a small circle consisting of 5 double, 1 purl, 3 double, fastened on to the button-hole stitch edging of the rosette, then 3 double, 1 purl, 5 double. Then turn the just-completed circle downwards, and afterwards work at a short distance a large circle consisting of 7 double, 6 times alternately 1 purl, 2 double, lastly 1 purl, 7 double, then 1 Josephine knot consisting of 7 plain. Then turn the work again, so that the last large circle is turned downwards, and repeat from * 12 times more; the large and small circles must be fastened on to one another, as seen in illustration. The fastening of the small circles on to the centre is likewise done from the illustration.

64.—*Cravat End in Tatting and Darned Netting.*

Materials: Messrs. Walter Evans and Co.'s tatting cotton No. 50; tatting-pin No. 3; square of netting; fine Mecklenburg thread No. 80.

64.—Cravat End in Tatting and Darned Netting.

The end of this cravat is ornamented with a square of darned netting, edged with a tatted border, and sewn on to the material of the cravat. But the diamond in tatting, or the square will look very pretty with this border. The square is worked in diamond netting, and has seven holes in length and breadth. They are darned in linen stitch, darning stitch, and *point d'esprit*, with Mecklenburg thread. The ground is worked over a mesh measuring three-tenths of an inch round. For each square one more row than is needed must be worked, and the cast-on stitches are cut off, as they are longer than the stitches of the other rows. The tatted border is worked with fine tatting cotton. Fasten the cotton at one corner of the square and work * a circle consisting of 7 double, 1 purl, then six times alternately 2 double, 1 purl, 7 double, fasten the cotton on to the same stitch of the ground where it was first fastened; #work a second circle like the first, but fasten it, instead of working the first purl on to the last purl of the preceding circle; fasten the cotton again on to the same stitch, then on to the next stitch, and work a small circle, consisting of 5 double fastened on to the last purl of the preceding circle, 4 double, 1 purl, 5 double. The cotton is fastened on to the same netted stitch as before, and then on to the next stitch; repeat twice more from #, and then repeat from * in all three times more, so that the square is edged all round. It is sewn into the material from the illustration.